IT AIN'T ME, BABE

Great Barrington Books

Bringing the old and new together in the spirit of W. E. B. Du Bois
∾ An imprint edited by Charles Lemert ∾

Titles Available

Keeping Good Time: Reflections on Knowledge, Power, and People
by Avery F. Gordon (2004)

Going Down for Air: A Memoir in Search of a Subject
by Derek Sayer (2004)

The Souls of Black Folk, 100th Anniversary Edition
by W. E. B. Du Bois, with commentaries by Manning Marable,
Charles Lemert, and Cheryl Townsend Gilkes (2004)

Sociology After the Crisis, Updated Edition
by Charles Lemert (2004)

Subject to Ourselves, by Anthony Elliot (2004)

The Protestant Ethic Turns 100
Essays on the Centenary of the Weber Thesis
edited by William H. Swatos, Jr., and Lutz Kaelber (2005)

Postmodernism Is Not What You Think
by Charles Lemert (2005)

Discourses on Liberation: An Anatomy of Critical Theory
by Kyung-Man Kim (2005)

Seeing Sociologically: The Routine Grounds of Social Action
by Harold Garfinkel, edited and introduced by Anne Warfield Rawls (2005)

The Souls of W. E. B. Du Bois
by Alford A. Young, Jr., Manning Marable, Elizabeth Higginbotham,
Charles Lemert, and Jerry G. Watts (2006)

Radical Nomad: C. Wright Mills and His Times
by Tom Hayden with Contemporary Reflections by Stanley Aronowitz,
Richard Flacks, and Charles Lemert (2006)

Critique for What? Cultural Studies, American Studies, Left Studies
by Joel Pfister (2006)

Social Solutions to Poverty, by Scott Meyers-Lipton (2006)

Everyday Life and the State, by Peter Bratsis (2006)

Thinking the Unthinkable: An Introduction to Social Theories
by Charles Lemert (2007)

Between Citizen and State: An Introduction to the Corporation
by David A. Westbrook (2007)

Politics, Identity, and Emotion, by Paul Hoggett (2009)

Out of Crisis: Rethinking Our Financial Markets, by David A. Westbrook
(2010)

Uncertain Worlds: World-Systems Analysis in Changing Times,
by Immanuel Wallerstein, Carlos Aguirre Rojas, and Charles Lemert (2012)

It Ain't Me, Babe: Bob Dylan and the Performance of Authenticity,
by Andrea Cossu (2012)

IT AIN'T ME, BABE

BOB DYLAN AND THE
PERFORMANCE OF AUTHENTICITY

ANDREA COSSU

Paradigm Publishers
Boulder • London

Copyright © 2012 Paradigm Publishers

Published in the United States by Paradigm Publishers, 5589 Arapahoe Avenue, Boulder, CO 80303 USA.

Paradigm Publishers is the trade name of Birkenkamp & Company, LLC, Dean Birkenkamp, President and Publisher.

Library of Congress Cataloging-in-Publication Data

Cossu, Andrea, 1975–
    It ain't me, babe: Bob Dylan and the performance of authenticity / Andrea Cossu.
        p. cm.
    Includes bibliographical references and index.
    ISBN 978-1-61205-187-1 (hardcover : alk. paper) —
ISBN 978-1-61205-188-8 (pbk. : alk. paper)
    1. Dylan, Bob, 1941—Criticism and interpretation. 2. Dylan, Bob, 1941—Performances. 3. Folk music—United States—History and criticism. 4. Popular music—History and criticism. I. Title.
    ML420.D98C69 2012
    782.42164092—dc23
                                                                              2012009981
Printed and bound in the United States of America on acid-free paper that meets the standards of the American National Standard for Permanence of Paper for Printed Library Materials.

Designed and Typeset by Straight Creek Bookmakers.

16 15 14 13 12   1 2 3 4 5

Contents

◇

Acknowledgments

I distinctly remember four of my "first" Dylan moments. There have been many others, but these have shaped my relationship with Dylan's work and have probably led to this book. I remember the first time I consciously heard Dylan's voice. It was 1984, and I was barely eight years old. I saw the video of *Jokerman,* and I recall my mother saying something like, "that is Bob Dylan," probably followed by something about "the minstrel of protest"; she knew little of what was going to happen in the years to come, including attending her first Dylan concert. I remember the first time I saw Dylan. Television journalists were on strike in my home country of Italy, and the Hard Rain concert replaced the midday news, with Dylan and Joan Baez strumming their acoustic guitars and performing a duet on "I Pity the Poor Immigrant" (strangely enough, this is the song that stuck in my mind). I remember the first time I saw Dylan in concert, on a stormy night in 1991, when I got the chance to hear both "A Hard Rain's A-Gonna Fall" (it was falling) and "Shelter from the Storm" (there was no shelter). Finally, I remember the first time I heard "Like a Rolling Stone." It was the summer of 1990, and one of my classmates had just bought the album *Highway 61 Revisited.* I listened, listened again, and rushed out to buy a copy, spending my pocket money for the week. I have shared my interest in Dylan with many people over the years, and many of them remember what they were doing or where they were the first time they heard "Like a Rolling Stone." One of my students once told me that every time is like the first time, but I tend to disagree: the first time, if Dylan's voice catches you by surprise, it leaves you speechless, breathless, and restless, and suddenly you realize you've been hooked.

This book is in part the ultimate result of a teenager's encounter with a singer and his songs. But even the chanciest things are shaped and guided through their realization. Many people have helped me with this project, by providing academic advice, editorial help, and the strong encouragement that only best friends and colleagues can give. This book has been made better because of their support and constructive criticism. I will forever be grateful to Charles Lemert, who has supported the project since he first heard about it and who has been my friend, colleague, and mentor. Most of all, he has taught me to never let my curiosity wane, because it is through our constant, curious use of the sociological imagination that we can make some sense of what we do as social scientists. Gary Alan Fine has been a source of inspiration with his writings on reputations, and his advice has helped improve many parts of this book, by pushing me to investigate things I had overlooked as well as to clarify several points; his support has been truly invaluable. Ron Eyerman helped make my stay at Yale a great experience, not the least for our early morning chats in front of our favorite coffeehouse. Ron is one of the many people I know who remembers the first time he heard "Like a Rolling Stone," so he knows what this book is all about. In Trento, and in many e-mails, Mario Diani has encouraged me to never give up, and I hope he takes this book as evidence that I didn't.

I developed this project while I was at Yale University, the University of New Haven, and the University of Padova: I thank Stuart Sidle and Raeleen Mautner at UNH, as well as Vered Vinitsky-Seroussi, Sarah Egan, Carolyn Ly, and Jeffrey Alexander. Parts of this book have been presented at the annual meeting of the American Sociological Association (Atlanta 2010) and the "Refractions of Bob Dylan" conference organized by the University of Vienna in 2011. I thank Wayne Brekhus and Eugen Banauch, as well as all the participants in those sessions. My editor at Paradigm, Dean Birkenkamp, has shown great enthusiasm for this project from the very beginning and has supported it through its completion. Working with him has been a real pleasure and a great professional experience. Many other people have helped me develop this project in several ways; I thank especially

Olof Bjoerner, who has done a wonderful job documenting Dylan's concerts and setlists; Baron and Michele Ulisse, for getting me a ticket when I needed it most; my students, junior colleagues, and friends, especially Shaina Hotchkiss, Francesco Galofaro, Loris Vergolini, Ester Cois, Renato Roda, Elena Pavan, Monica Soldà, Elena Kyrianova, Maeve Pearson, Giulia Peron, Nadine Amalfi, Jason Mast, Divya Vaid, Gulay Turkmen, Chiara Rossi, and Aurora Mandara. Finally, I want to thank the good people who have traveled with me. Waverly Duck and I have talked little about this project, but a lot about many other things; he was always there when I was in need, taking the positive role, when I was being negative, and he was always able to make me more positive. With Matteo Bortolini, I have shared many conversations about the social dynamic of success, as well as the occasional good pint of beer, in New Haven, Boston, San Francisco, Padova, and Bologna; he has been the best informal reviewer I could find, and I hope he did not mind listening to my ramblings about the virtues of the Never Ending Tour. Tullia Dymarz used to sketch her math theorems while I was drafting an earlier version of the first two chapters, and this remains a very precious image to me. I hope she learned something about Dylan and that she will forgive me if I didn't learn anything about math or Leonard Cohen. Isabella Araldi has always shown me the value of her deep friendship in absence, silence, and distance—best friends do not need to talk. My parents, Grazia and Salvatore, have been through the ordeal of having a son who is a Dylan fan; despite that, they have been my greatest fans and supporters, in countless ways. Finally, there is Silvia, because suddenly I turned around, and she was standing there. This book is for her.

◇

Introduction

When Bob Dylan entered Columbia Studio A to record his first, eponymous album, it was November 1961, and he had just turned twenty. He looked young and scruffy, but he had allegedly lived many lives. Some of them had already been sealed and become part of the past before his arrival in New York, just a few months earlier. He had been a child reared in a Jewish, middle-class family in Minnesota; a daydreamer who spent his adolescence writing poetry, playing guitar and piano, or listening to country and western music; a teenage greaser who led badly rehearsed rock-and-roll bands, and whose main ambition was to "join Little Richard," as he wrote in his high school yearbook; a piano player for a famous act of the time, the kind of sideman who ultimately does not get the gig; a freshman and soon-to-be college dropout, at the University of Minnesota, where he discovered the outsider-ness of folk music in the clubs of the Dinkytown district of Minneapolis, the Twin Cities' response to the much more bohemian Greenwich Village; and a youngster who, very early on, decided to change his name and model a new persona. Those lives, however, had been lived by Robert Zimmerman, and becoming "Bob Dylan" was perhaps one more act of creation, deception, and imagination.

Bob Dylan's biography had been, by all measures, much more turbulent. He was an outcast, rather than a dropout. He had left home at a young age; he was, perhaps, an orphan whose whereabouts could be anywhere between Minnesota and North or South Dakota; he had worked in a circus; he had learned the blues during hard traveling times in the company of a number of black singers, who passed down to him (as an act of acceptance and recognition) their chords and lyrics. He had crisscrossed the country in imitation of his idol, a folksinger, writer, columnist, and radio personality whose name was Woody Guthrie.

Guthrie, perhaps, was one of the very few things that Dylan and Zimmerman had in common. Woody Guthrie had done all the things that Robert Zimmerman had imagined for his alter ego's concocted biography. Guthrie came from an impoverished middle-class family in Oklahoma; he had hit the road during the Great Depression, jumping on boxcars and living the life of a hobo; he had sung for pennies just to cheer up and mobilize the poor, almost desperate, audiences of Okies, who had been forced to move to California; he had been a political organizer and a witty columnist for communist newspapers during the New Deal and the years of the Popular Front; he had written (or adapted, or stolen, or re-owned) hundreds of songs and a cult book, *Bound for Glory*; he had merged the tradition of American folk music with political activism, following in the footsteps of Joe Hill, singing about a land that was your land, modern-day Robin Hoods like Pretty Boy Floyd, Jesse James, and a Jesus Christ who would have probably joined the International Workers of the World, vigilante men, and Tom Joad, straight out of *The Grapes of Wrath*. Unlike Zimmerman, Woodrow Wilson Guthrie had not radically changed his name. Like Zimmerman, however, he had tried to hide himself under a veil of authenticity, while simultaneously creating new meanings for the term *authenticity* and contributing—in different ways —to the narrative that centers around the folksinger as both a narrator and a hero (Kennedy 2009; Rodnitzky 1988).

Dylan's move to New York was both a quest for success in the circles of the folk scene, which was blooming at the time, and a more private search for Guthrie—who at the time was hospitalized in New Jersey, progressively incapacitated by Huntington's chorea, a rare genetic disease that ultimately claimed his life in 1967. It took Dylan less than a week to meet his idol and make his first amateur appearance on a stage in Greenwich Village. It took three months to get his first professional booking and a little more than a year to record and finally release his first album. Things went fast, and they got even faster when Dylan became the voice of the folk revival—to some the voice of his generation, to others the new voice of the youth who were rallying for civil rights and desegregation and hoping for a new frontier. It was enough, in other words, to be and be perceived as a poet, a revolutionary, a prophet, and ultimately an artist who (as I write) has traveled a journey through fame that has spanned five decades.

There have been as many Bob Dylans over these fifty years as there were in the months when he was creating "Bob Dylan." Maybe he did not escape from home at "10, 12, 13, 15, 15½, 17 an' 18. I been caught an' brought back all but once,"[1] as he once claimed, but the general perception is that Dylan has tried restlessly to escape his myth, his audience, and the stories planted in the press. It has been a journey through fame, but also a journey made of surprises, turning points, detours, controversies, and praises that have shaped the public perception of the artist and his work.

The idea of a "shape-shifting" Dylan that has resulted from all these changes, indeed, is almost reassuring in its familiarity with our commonsense perception of genius and talent. Scholars and critics, as well as fans, have often referred to the archetypical figure of Proteus, the shape-shifting god, to describe the personae that Dylan has embodied during his career. Just as Proteus was able to transform himself into a lion, a serpent, a leopard, a pig, water, and trees, Dylan has been folk icon, rock star, country crooner, waning act ready for a Las Vegas casino, preacher warning that the new Apocalypse would bring fire, not water, aged idol in leather pants, and the leader of a cowboy band that seems to have come to town straight from a Mississippi steamer. Sometimes one gets the impression that the "Bob Dylan" we see is a Bob Dylan impersonator who approaches the idol-like figure with a sarcastic twist. Nowhere have this protean construction of his own figure and the reconstruction of Bob Dylan as a Proteus-like figure been clearer than in Todd Haynes's movie *I'm Not There*, where six different actors, including a woman playing the androgynous Dylan of the mid-1960s and an African American kid playing the Guthrie-esque Dylan who manufactured his biography, are needed to describe some of the transformations that Dylan went through during his career (MacDonald 2009; Smith 2010). It almost seems that, to understand Dylan—one of the most important products of popular culture—we need an archetype that predates history and has its feet firmly set on the muddy ground of myth; as Benedict Giamo has argued, Dylan's style is a "protean style" of reinvention, where the artist is always on the move and where the paradox of a protean "original" state leads to "an abiding sense of openness and indeterminacy, a return not to what is stable and familiar—a homecoming—but to possibility, to reinvention, to the contention between being and becoming" (Giamo 2011, 1).

Suggestive as it is, and very effective, the notion of a "protean" Dylan can be complemented by the sociological vision of the artist and his fame, which I would like to develop in this book. If we follow the myth, we notice that Proteus is always in an ambivalent state—liminal by nature, he intentionally transforms himself, but this transformation must be performed and recognized in public. A witness needs to be involved, establishing a circle of recognition and perception that goes from the artist to the audience and back. In other words, the construction of talent and genius (even in the most renowned cases like Dylan's) is always embedded in social interactions that shape the public perception of an artist, which is created very often against and beyond the latter's intentions. Thus, when we read that Dylan is "a moving target, unwilling to be pinned down"—as scholar David Yaffe has argued (Yaffe 2011, xix)—this should not come as a surprise, because the unpredictability of the meanings that artists have for their publics is what constitutes—at least in part—their aura. Dylan, or for that matter any other figure that has achieved the public status of "genius," seems more the result of these social interactions, cooperations, and struggles to define the artist, than a projection that radiates from the artist to his audiences.

What I would like to discuss is the interplay of social and cultural factors that has shaped our contemporary image of Bob Dylan (so fragmented and unidimensional at the same time). This sociological vision is counterintuitive: Indeed, isn't Dylan the visionary who "forced folk into bed with rock" almost singlehandedly? The artist who rewrote the rules of popular music and songwriting? The one—the only one—who has ever been considered for the Nobel Prize in Literature? These are remarkable achievements, which testify to Dylan's peculiar position at the intersection of high culture and popular culture. But in singling Dylan out, they also silence the complex context in which his star originally rose, the reasons for the ups and downs of his career, and the cultural motives that lie behind Dylan's resurrection as an artist and icon over the past fifteen years or so. What we are left with is a Dylan myth—a complex social text—that echoes the notion of the Romantic genius as an independent source of his own seductive power and isolates the artist from the contexts of production and reception, which pose powerful constraints and open equally powerful opportunities for the emergence, consolidation, and transformation of the artistic reputation as a "genius."

Dylan's quite unique position in the field of popular culture has been established by what I would call a "regime of high visibility," coproduced by the artist, the audience, and myriad powerful intermediaries, who have created "Dylan" as an icon, a star, and, to some extent, even a brand. There have been times where Dylan has been extraordinarily visible (like, for instance, in 1965–1966, 1974, or even today, when one can get the chance to see him play just around the corner). And there have been times when Dylan was— quite ironically—visible as a ghost, through his very absence: Woodstock in 1969 (he was not there, he was staging his Hank Williams persona at the Isle of Wight Festival) or at San Francisco's Warfield Theatre in 1979, when the man was on stage, but the Dylan people knew was nowhere to be found, diminished by his sudden decision to perform only new songs that resulted from his conversion to Christianity. And there was a problematically absent/present Dylan in the years that preceded his revival of the late 1990s, when the so-called Never Ending Tour was a nightly exercise in the deconstruction and reassembly of "Bob Dylan," through radically different, brilliant or lackluster, arrangements of his immense discography.

This tension between absence and presence leads to an important point. Quite ironically, for a star whose trademark has often been a combination of elusiveness and self-reclusion, Dylan has constructed his aura—with a great help from his audience—by acting on stage, by being visible and performing his visibility on the stage, no matter if it was for a 2,000-seat theater or the huge crowds of Blackbushe 1978, Live Aid 1985, Saugerties-Woodstock 1994, or Bologna 1997, when he played before an ailing Pope John Paul II.

There is, in other words, a centrality of performance that has often been overlooked in the consideration of the social construction of Dylan's fame. Among Dylan's boldest career moves were "going electric" at Newport (which I will consider in Chapter 2), and "going gospel" at the Warfield in 1979. Both were anticipated on record, but they made little sense (and people even thought that he was not that serious about plugging in or preaching about the Lord) until he performed on stage. Those turning points had to be dramatized in order to become part of the public perception of Dylan as an artist. Moreover, it often goes unnoticed—or taken for granted—that Dylan is always experienced through performance, be it the recorded performance of "Like a Rolling Stone," as it was sung and played in June 1965, or the lesser-known performance of "Shelter from the Storm" in Milan, 1994, which I had the privilege to witness, my hands firmly on the rail. I have been playing the recording of that performance recently in order to relive the sensations I felt while I was there as well as to spark some new ones.

To anticipate some of the conclusions of this book, our consumption of stars and icons (and Dylan certainly is one of them) requires to some extent that the artist embody his aura, something that philosopher Walter Benjamin described masterfully as "a distance as close as it can be" (Benjamin 2008). There is a conflict born of this necessity to embody the artistic aura, in that the artist is required to create and reinforce the mystery of his distance, his inaccessibility to his audience, while at the same time reducing this distance in the play between artist and audience, which creates a feeling of proximity whereby the audience feels that they "know" and even "own" the artist.

In the domain of popular music, this whole process is guided by performance. Artists are something more than their image, but it is true that they are also something more than their sound and voice. Although our consumption of singers tends to be centered on recorded performances, there is always a space when they become more available and visible, and this is when they perform for an audience, proving on stage that they can be trusted as competent artists, in control of their voices and instruments. Given the importance of live performance in the evaluation of rock's authenticity (Auslander 1998, 2004), the moments when artists appear on stage are crucial moments, when they project to the public some concrete sense that they are exactly who they claim to be and have the competence to sing, play, and move as rock artists.

But performance is never a one-way flow of communication from the artist to the audience. It requires reciprocity and, most of all, the interaction that makes distance "as close as it can be." It is through performance (and through reaction to that performance) that an audience comes to experience the feeling of appropriation of an artist, a kind of fusion between two otherwise separate worlds. This process—which establishes a series of dialogues between artists and publics and between each of them and the broader culture in which they are immersed and which makes appreciation and appropriation possible—is ultimately one of the foundations on which artistic reputation stands. The artist, in other words, is made, not only of a fixed, iconic raw stuff, but also—and predominantly—of what he communicates through performance and, to some extent, of his acting as a performer—the "performance of a performance" (Frith 1996, 211), which often requires the adoption of a persona that is in an intermediate position between the artist's subjectivity and the characters he brings to life in the performance of his songs.

The focus of this book—on Dylan as performer and Dylan on stage—results from these reflections about the dramaturgical nature of the process of construction and reproduction of "genius." In a case like Dylan's, where his words are often perceived to be as important as his music, and the traces of his text as more important than the actual encounter with the artist, my choice seems both odd and promising.[2] Whereas some authors have stressed the importance of the dimension of performance (Bowden 1982; Day 1988; Williams 1994, 2004a, 2004b), they have seldom followed up from an analytical point of view about performance in all its dramatic and theatrical dynamics. Rather, analyses tend to go back to the perceived centrality of Dylan's texts and do not approach Dylan with the analytic tools of performance theory, with all its interdisciplinary vocabulary that centers on the symbolic and practical aspects of life and action.

The five chapters of this book deal primarily with four important tours and live experiences in Dylan's career: the making of Bob Dylan's reputation in the context of the folk revival of the early 1960s (Chapter 1); the electric turn of 1965–1966 (Chapter 2); the Rolling Thunder Revue of 1975 –1976 (Chapter 3); the Gospel Tour of 1979–1980 (Chapter 4); and finally the ongoing project of the Never Ending Tour (a label grudgingly disowned by Dylan and problematically accepted by the fans and the press) that has occupied the last decades of Dylan's career, starting in 1988 (Chapter 5).

Every chapter is also an exploration of both the dynamics that regulate the making of fame and the role that culture plays in the production of artistic reputation, especially that part of artistic reputation that is more closely related with the performance and the perception of authenticity. The relationship among performance, reputation, and the creation of authenticity is the thread that links the chapters together. The academic debate on these themes has spread in the past decades across the humanities and the social sciences, but here I would like to take a more direct focus on the ways Dylan embodies authenticity, and on the way his performance of authenticity exposes him to critical evaluation and changes in his image and reputation. People have debated Dylan's authenticity for decades, and critics, audiences, fellow artists, and scholars have variously declared him to be authentic or "fake." Yet the reasons Dylan is perceived to be authentic and the reasons audiences align with the way he performs or declares his own authenticity have often remained obscure, buried in narratives about his individual talent. I argue that Dylan has been successful in embodying a perception of authenticity that comes from the margins of US vernacular culture, and he has been able to reach a synthesis between these features of authenticity and the debate about originality and creativity that constitutes much public discourse about art. The very existence of these debates and controversies highlights the relational, and interactional, aspects of artistic identity and authenticity (Becker 1982), the fact that artists are less the outcome of objective qualities of their selves or their songs and more the result of what they and other actors do—cooperating or competing—for the creation of their image as artists. What is interesting is the depth, extension, and precarious balance of this collective work and the part it plays in the definition of authenticity.

Be it about Dylan's relationship to collective American memories, the exploration of the dynamics of his success, or the clashes of genres, there is a complex environment into which Dylan's authenticity is made, unmade, and remade. This environment is the seemingly "soft" stuff of culture, emotions, and expectations in which the artist is never a product of his own moves, but always a product of his relationship —within culture and sometimes against culture—with his publics, who constantly struggle to get close to the artist, while keeping him distant enough to allow his mystery to keep rolling on. Performance reveals this dynamic, and looking at performance is less a way to narrate the myth than to debunk the routes through which that myth is produced and embodied.

Notes

1. On April 12, 1963, Dylan performed an important concert at New York City's Town Hall and ended the show by reciting a poem entitled "Last Thoughts on Woody Guthrie," which essentially closes the folk-revivalist phase of his early career. For the concert, Dylan wrote another free-form poem, "My Life in a Stolen Moment," a long, semiautobiographical piece that juxtaposes snippets of his childhood in Duluth with the manufactured tall tales that he had produced in the Village as a means to create his image of authenticity. The image of Dylan as a runaway is a key aspect of this poem.

2. There have been so many books on Dylan's lyrics that it is almost impossible to provide a comprehensive bibliography here. However, in addition to the ones that are discussed in this book, the reader might want to check several publications that focus mostly on Dylan's written words and recorded works, like Burns (2008), Gill (2011), Heine (2009), Muir (2003), Pichaske (2010), Ricks (2003), Riley (1992), and Smith (2002), Vernezze and Porter (2006), as well as the many, more scholarly publications that I critically review in the following chapters.

ONE

I Ain't No Prophet

Becoming Bob Dylan in the Folk Revival

On November 19, 2001, Bob Dylan's tour made its yearly stop in New York. He was playing the Madison Square Garden Arena, and his latest album, *"Love and Theft,"* had been released a little more than two months earlier, on 9/11—the day New York became a wounded city. Many reviewers found a prophetic tone in Dylan's lyrics, which seemed to come from a timeless territory, where Dylan had met the ghosts of countless blues singers, with their references to a "sky full of fire, pain pourin' down," to "bags full of dead men's bones," and to "the shacks [that] are slidin' down, Folks lose their possessions, folks are leaving town."[1] In the audience, few noticed that the date was close to the fortieth anniversary of the recording of Dylan's first album (on November 20, 1961), just a few blocks away from Madison Square Garden. It almost seemed that, at least temporarily, things had gone full circle and that Dylan was back where he belonged. He acknowledged it, overcoming his notorious reluctance to speak from the stage, in a heartfelt homage to New York, "Most of these songs were written here and the ones that weren't were recorded here. You don't have to ask me how I feel about this town."[2]

Dylan had come to New York as a stranger, in the sense German sociologist Georg Simmel meant at the turn of the twentieth century, as someone "who comes today and stays tomorrow," a potential wanderer who "has not quite over-come the freedom of coming and going" (1950, 402). Dylan's first road trip to New York in the winter of 1961, "across the country from the Midwest in a four-door sedan, '57 Impala —straight out of Chicago, clearing the hell out of there" (Dylan 2004b, 8), was a Grand Tour with a one-way ticket, a bohemian *Bildungsreise*. His ultimate goal was existential, which made it more likely that he was bound to become the kind of stranger described by Simmel: "It wasn't money or love"—Dylan recalled in his autobiography—"that I was looking for," but rather something different:

> I was there to find singers, the ones I'd heard on record—Dave Van Ronk, Peggy Seeger, Ed McCurdy, Brownie McGhee and Sonny Terry, Josh White, the New Lost City Ramblers, Reverend Gary Davis and a bunch of others—most of all to find Woody Guthrie. New York City, the city that would come to shape my destiny. Modern Gomorrah. I was at the initiation point of square one but in no sense a neophyte. (Dylan 2004b, 9)

Dylan was right: he had already been initiated into folk music and its alternative pantheon during his Minnesota days in Hibbing and in the Twin Cities. There, however, he had also been under the spell of Little Richard, Jimmie Rodgers, Hank Williams, Howlin' Wolf, and those rhythm and blues singers whom he listened to late at night, when the air was clean and the radio waves were able to reach Hibbing—yes, even Hibbing, up north and close to the Canadian border.[3] The blues, rock and roll, country music, and folk; by the time he got to New York, Dylan had already soaked himself in the music he was going to explore in the decades to come.

Any reconstruction of "what" happened afterward cannot be merely biographical, for it has had a larger impact on our perception of popular music and in general on the culture of that seminal decade to which Dylan seems forever to be linked: "It is what Dylan sang, said, did, and represented for a few years in the 1960s that continues to draw the public's attention and ignite the imagination of new generations of listeners" (Masur 2007, 166). To some extent, the approach has also to be sociological, and the "what" becomes a "why," which is even more difficult to answer. Why did Bob Dylan, who was just a twenty-year-old former student, with no remarkable career in show business, limited vocal skills, limited ability as a guitar player, and (at that time) a very limited and uninteresting songbook, end up being one of the few artists in a league of his own, to the point that he can claim—without being ridiculed—that he "owns" the sixties (Lethem 2006), no matter how reluctant he has been or is?

The answer lies in an analysis of the rules of a particular game, the folk music revival and the process of *becoming* a folksinger, which was governed by a very peculiar logic. Furthermore, one has also to consider the tensions that rose the moment the folk revival was undergoing a sort of coming of age crisis, when artists where crossing over to larger audiences and were met by greater and greater recognition and commercial success. If we want to understand Dylan's role in the sixties and his rise to fame, we cannot ignore the insight that comes from both his peculiar artistic trajectory and the wider sociocultural and institutional context in which he was embedded from the time of his arrival in New York and which influenced the creation of his reputation.

In the next two chapters, I will consider the process that led to the electric turn (Dylan famously "going electric" at the Newport Folk Festival) and the reasons a controversial process, like the transition from folk, to folk-rock, to rock, which was initially marked by heated, critical debate and charges of Dylan's "selling out," became a foundational moment for contemporary popular culture. If we assume that "going electric" was not a decision made on the spot (as sometimes the mythology constructed about Dylan claims), but rather the outcome of a long process of reconfiguration of the coalitions that had emerged in the folk revival in the preceding years, then focusing on the folk revival, the role it assigned to artists, and its interaction with the larger field of popular and vernacular culture helps debunk the charismatic narrative that has been constructed around Dylan (according to which Dylan's success is only a consequence of his natural talent and qualities).[4] It also helps clarify the interaction of stylistic, political, and performance motives that governed Dylan's transition to rock and the creation of rock music as a totally new arena for debate, production, and consumption.

Hard Times in New York Town: The Institutional Context of the Folk Revival

Histories of the American folk revival usually recount how early twentieth century interest in the cultural preservation of ancient forms of popular culture, coming from an idealized society had been transformed, since the 1920s, by the encounter with progressive politics, communist-style (Cantwell 1996; Cohen 2002; Filene 2000). The turn to the strategy of the Popular Front, following the 7th Congress of the Communist International in 1935, meant a "nationalization" of the cultural politics of Communist parties all over the world, but it proved to be particularly successful in the United States, where the Communist Party of the USA connected itself to a broader national tradition (Ottanelli 1991, 83–136). The interest for folk song, as something that was perceived to come from the people and opposed to music written and performed in order to educate the people to higher, more modernist aesthetic standards, rose in this context; as sociologists Ron Eyerman and Andrew Jameson have argued in their study on music and social movements, the Popular Front "expressed its collective identity not merely through political tracts and strikes and demonstrations, but also, and perhaps more significantly, through art, music, and ritual" (Eyerman and Jamison 1998, 65).

There was, in other words, an expressive side of political mobilization, which centered on the people as subjects of culture and "realism" as an aesthetic manifesto (Vials 2009), rather than simply as a recipient of political inculcation. Songs were sung, adapted, rewritten, but most of all, they showed how a native American culture (or the progressive vision with deep roots in a tradition of American nativism and populism) could become a part of the Left's understanding of what America was and ought to be. This influence was enduring, able to extend its reach well beyond the abandonment of the political strategy, crossing decades and generations, and even surviving the Red Scare and the years of McCarthyism. The folk revival that was shaped in those years was thus a project with different meanings, in which tensions were generated by the merging of a political strategy with an interest for a "real" or imagined national tradition. Was the folk revival a cultural project or a social movement? What was the relationship of its protagonists to the people? What were the dominant ideas about its cultural goals, and how did they relate to the wider system of cultural production and consumption in American society?

None of these questions ever received an unambiguous answer in the context of the folk revival, which was fragmented by a series of internal cleavages that—in the last instance—articulated two major themes: the value of tradition and the role of authenticity. These two themes contributed to the definition of different "politics of style," which the most relevant cultural entrepreneurs of the revival framed in an attempt to provide a unitary vision of politics, aesthetics, ideology, and style. To some extent, tradition and authenticity were fabricated fantasies about "the other," which resulted in the appropriation of cultural forms and in their hybridization for a public that was yearning for a means to reduce the social fractures that were harming American society across racial, generational, and cultural lines.

Both *tradition* and *authenticity* are key terms for understanding Dylan's trajectory and the cultural factors that shaped his reputation as an artist. However, Dylan always positioned himself in a complex manner vis-à-vis the value of tradition and authenticity. Rather than creating their meanings anew, his artistic trajectory was influenced from the very beginning by the meanings they had in his reference community, that of revivalists, especially the urban revivalists who were prominent on the New York scene. I will review some of the reasons these two themes were central in the context of the folk revival and then analyze the way the young Bob Dylan created and performed his own authenticity.

Framing Tradition in the Folk Revival

Revivalist movements must always cope with the paradoxical nature of the tradition they refer to. To some extent, a tradition is always "invented," as historians Eric Hobsbawm and Terence Ranger have argued in a seminal study (Hobsbawm and Ranger 1983): "where possible, [traditions] normally attempt to establish continuity with a suitable historic past. . . . However, insofar as there is such reference to a historic past, the peculiarity of 'invented' traditions is that the continuity with it is largely fictitious. In short, they are responses to novel situations which take the form of reference to old situations, or which establish their own past by quasi-obligatory repetition" (Hobsbawm and Ranger 1983, 1). A tradition is invented because artifacts produced in the present might have no clear counterpart in the distant past to which they are claimed to belong; and a tradition is invented because relevant portions of a real or imagined past are "traditionalized" by interested parties, entrepreneurs, and cultural policymakers, for instrumental or economic reasons or as an element in the collective creation of nostalgia. It is not surprising, then, that the debate on tradition always took a central position in the folk revival, as a trait that unified the political activists of the 1930s to the bohemian urban revivalists of the late 1950s, out of which Dylan emerged.

One of the positions that had always been present in the study of folk music rejected this present-oriented, instrumental vision of tradition and favored a notion based on a series of distances (cultural and temporal) that created the realm of tradition as something untouched by subsequent processes of "traditionalization" and modernization. In 1954, right at the dawn of the second wave of the American Folk Revival, the International Folk Music Council made the criteria for qualifying a song as a true heritage of "the folk" explicit, echoing older formulations by prominent folklorists like Francis James Child and Cecil Sharp. Folk music, the Council argued, "is the product of a musical tradition that has been evolved through the process of oral transmission. The factors that shape the tradition are: 1) continuity which links the present with the past; 2) variation which springs from the creative impulse of the individual or the group; 3) selection by the community which determines the form or forms in which the music survives" (quoted in Bluestein 1994, 22). "Real" folk music, in other words, could come only from an oral culture as the result of a process of transmission. In this process, folk music was the music that remained pure and untouched by the external influences of a world where music, like many other cultural artifacts, was produced and consumed as a commodity: "The term [*folk music*] can be applied to music that has been evolved from rudimentary beginnings by a community uninfluenced by popular and art music, and it can likewise be applied to music which is originated with an individual composer and has subsequently been absorbed into the unwritten living tradition of a community" (quoted in Bluestein 1994, 22). According to this definition, songs like "Barbara Allen" qualify as folk songs, as do popular songs that have entered the oral tradition, like Stephen Foster's "Hard Times," which Dylan recorded for his "traditional" and "folk" album *Good As I Been to You* in 1992. But under the same criteria, choosing whether Robert Johnson's "Crossroads" or the Mississippi Sheiks' "Blood in My Eyes" (both copyrighted recordings made and released commercially) are instances of "folk song" may prove much more difficult.

The difficulty arose from the persistence of a myth: that, as Benjamin Filene has argued, the research and collecting activity of folklorists was affected by a prejudice that excluded all forms of vernacular culture that had been touched (even only marginally) by modernity. It also excluded other forms of vernacular expression that did not belong to a nativist canon, most importantly that of the African American culture. In their vision, a folk song was as "an extremely old song, usually a ballad, that had originated from Great Britain and was currently sung by rural, isolated, mountain people who were white, Anglo-Saxon protestant" (Filene 2000, 26). However, even in the early twentieth century those areas were rapidly modernizing, and only the most isolated households could claim to fit into the categories that earlier folklorists had envisaged, not to mention the generations of "class mutineers" and romantic rebels who—from Pete Seeger, to Ramblin' Jack Elliot, Bob Dylan, and Joan Baez—came from a more urban, middle-class background, but aligned to the values coming from a perceived "Other" and lived the Romance of the Outsider, "the belief that people somehow marginal to society possess cultural values and resources missing among other Americans" (Hale 2011, 1).

This myth of the outsider was political as well as aesthetic. Indeed, the roster of folk revivalists cum activists who were bred in the Popular Front years rejected many of the premodern criteria that still guided academic research on folklore and turned to a more political, and open, vision of the "folk process"; they did not fear the cultural contact and the adaptation of folk songs to present conditions, a practice that was as old as British broadside ballads and that had already been exploited by Joe Hill and other Wobbly organizers. Old gospels could become picket line chants; the melody of a hymn could be appropriated for a topical song; lines from the blues could be reassembled, grafting a technique from those blues singers who played in juke joints. The folk process, indeed, was less about the preservation of purity and more about the acknowledgment that change is what creates the folk, as Pete Seeger, among others, has claimed:

> There are many definitions of folk music, but the one which makes most sense to me is the one that says it is not simply a group of old songs. Rather, it is a process, which has been going on for thousands of years, in which ordinary people re-create the old music, changing it a little here and there as their lives change. (Seeger 1965, in De Turk and Poulin 1967, 48)

The New York folk scene, since the 1930s, had been shaped by these ideas about tradition, which were still dominant when Dylan came to town. Dylan has always moved within the loose boundaries of the folk process, grabbing and chewing pieces of song in an endless series of commutations and reworkings. Certainly he came to a scene where the folk-process, with its indulgence on appropriation and the much more questionable practice of copyrighting songs whose origin could not be traced (as cultural entrepreneurs like collector Alan Lomax and record label owner Moses Asch did systematically), defined both the tradition in which one moved and what was deemed traditional and what was not. In this context, the second key concept of the folk revival—authenticity—played an even bigger role.

Creating Authenticity in the Folk Revival

Folk music had never circulated entirely within the "folk," and many of the performers who came to be recognized as the epitome of folk music belonged either to a totally different class sector of American society or were not impervious to the influences of popular culture. Even many of the singers who—like Leadbelly and Mississippi John Hurt—were perceived as most rooted in tradition, as relics of a distant and pure past (and who were branded and marketed as such), were equally comfortable with chain gang songs and religious hymns, Tin Pan Alley music and self-penned compositions that adapted popular tunes (Ratcliffe 2011). Not to mention the icon of the two revivals, Woody Guthrie. More than the carriers of a tradition untouched by modernity, folksingers needed to be "authentic" in order to be recognized by their peers and their public. The notion of authenticity—even more negotiable than the notion of tradition—was seen as the key to keeping the vision of tradition embodied by artists who were not—in most cases—part of "the folk" attuned to their imaginary community of reference and allowed them to produce claims about their purity. "Authenticity" always had a normative effect, because singers were required to prove they were authentic and adapt to the external demands of their peers. Authenticity was considered a means to acquire legitimacy and was the most important characteristic a folksinger could exhibit so as not to be dismissed as "fake" (Redhead and Street 1989).

However, authenticity was as socially constructed and imagined as ideas about the folk were. Was Woody Guthrie "authentic," even though he came from an impoverished middle-class family, had made several attempts to achieve commercial success, and always struggled between his rambling hobo lifestyle and his ambitions to cross over to wider audiences (Kaufman 2011; Klein 1999)? Was Leadbelly "authentic" when he came to New York following the Lomaxes and was somewhat forced to wear a prisoner's uniform to stress his "outsiderness"? Was McKinley Morganfield "authentic" when, after being recorded by the Lomaxes on one of their numerous trips to collect "original" folk songs, he migrated north to Chicago and started pioneering the electric blues, using a stage name, Muddy Waters, which led him to achieve legendary status (Filene 2000, 76–132)? Hybridization and stylistic transformation were as much a part of the practice of authenticity as nostalgic reference to tradition was. Yet the "cult of authenticity," as historian Benjamin Filene has labeled it, could not have emerged without the compromises and efforts of cultural brokers like record executives, folk enthusiasts, critics, fanzine editors, and fellow singers. All these players—movement entrepreneurs, who in most cases were aiming at both political mobilization and the fixation of progressive aesthetic boundaries (Roy 2010)—interacted with the individual artists, constructing a network of activities that served two functions: they provided opportunities for artists to achieve the status of semiprofessional or professional performer, and they exercised widespread control of the artists, setting the standards with which a folksinger needed to comply, in order to be perceived as "authentic."

Authenticity was a multivocal concept, despite all attempts to reify its cultural and social referents. Often conceived to be in contraposition to commercialism, the social meanings of authentic changed from one generation to another, and "authentic" folk songs—the ones played to death by all the young protagonists of the urban revival of the 1960s—were those that had been considered either residual or inauthentic by their stepparents on the scene and the highbrow folklorists who had set the standards of academic folklore studies. Learning from Harry Smith's *Anthology of American Folk Music* was nothing less than a rite of passage for many of those young folksingers. Yet, for the most part, those recordings were included because they were available as a result of their having been originally recorded and produced with commercial goals in mind. They were records that were supposed to sell, and not relics of a romantic, pure, and traditional past.[5]

However, this modified notion of authenticity did not greatly affect the key connotations and practices associated with "being authentic" in the context of the revival. Discussing the patronizing John Lomax's construction of Leadbelly as an authentic folksinger, Filene stresses that "revival audiences yearn to identify with folk figures, but identification is premised on difference. Roots musicians are expected to be premodern, unrestrainedly emotive, and noncommercial" (Filene 2000, 63). The dialectic between modernity and tradition was solved in an unbalanced way in the production of authenticity, yet the presentation of authenticity was always fabricated and filtered through a set of cultural assumptions that were essentially modern and politically progressive. Artists were required to perform their authenticity as a means to gain recognition, but this performance usually put them in contact with the most fundamental riddle of authenticity: being authentic was a strategy that artists in the folk revival adopted in order to make themselves distinct and visible, focusing on their individuality in a subculture that stressed, contrarily, communitarian values. Although this dialectic between individuality and collectivistic assumptions had always shaped the claims about authenticity in the folk revival, when Dylan came onto the scene, the game had become considerably more complicated. Commercial forces were trying to exploit the folk revival, and artists were, for their part, willing to adapt to the demands of commercialism, either by surrendering to them or rationalizing their attempt to enter a larger circuit as a means to introduce folk music to a larger public. Yet, in the process, the difficult task was to project authenticity to audiences that had not been socialized to the game of authenticity, as it was played in the more restricted circles of the folk revival. This tension affected Dylan from the very beginning, and he was involved in defining a "hard-core" vision of authenticity that could appeal to larger audiences. During this process, Dylan's status as a prominent artist was created, in cooperation and competition among artists and other figures, in a fluid and changing network.

The Young Dylan and the Performance of Authenticity

Like many others, Dylan had to *learn* how to be authentic, yet his own vision of authenticity, which he had started to craft in Minneapolis, did not necessarily meet the demanding standards set in Greenwich Village. Although the scene of Greenwich Village was organized around a hierarchy of clubs and coffeehouses, and young newcomers could easily find a stage for their performances, aesthetic boundaries still worked to keep them at the margins in case their constructed style did not conform to the formal and informal rules that regulated the life of a folksinger in the Village. Dylan, on his part, was perceived as too rough even for a scene that encouraged amateurs to take the stage and showcase their (sometimes limited) skills. He sounded, as was recalled in an early song, "like a hillbilly," when folk clubs and coffeehouses wanted "folksingers."

According to Dylan, this scene took place in one of those "coffee-houses on the block." It was probably the Cafe Wha?, a "subterranean cavern, liquorless, ill lit, low ceiling, like a wide dining hall with chairs and tables—opened at noon, closed at four in the morning" (Dylan 2004b, 8). It was just one of many places that were cashing in on folk music and the endless stream of performers who were struggling to make it in a competitive scene. Dylan has described them as "nameless and miserable, low-level basket houses or small coffeehouses where the performer passed the hat. But I began to play as many as I could. I had no choice" (Dylan 2004b, 16). And even in these places his ragged, nasal voice was met with no favor: "[Fred Neil, master of ceremonies at the Cafe Wha?] asked me to play something. After about a minute, he said I could play harmonica with him during his sets" (Dylan 2004b, 8).

These coffeehouses were lion's dens, first steps in a career trajectory that many folksingers experienced only within the boundaries of the Village and that could lead—if one were lucky, connected, and bold enough—to gigs in better and better clubs and a record deal, which could, in turn, mean an improvement in the singer's position, allowing them to play larger clubs, or even concert halls, for the very few who became national stars. Even though they were perceived by many as performers' ghettoes, the coffeehouses represented an opportunity to trade songs, make connections, and learn how to be on stage. Together with other venues (the Sunday meetings at Washington Square, the hootenannies in clubs and apartments, and gigs in the better clubs, or everyone's hangout place—the Folklore Center run by Izzy Young), the coffeehouses were part of a hierarchical system of venues that offered the opportunity for semiprofessional singers to be nurtured by more experienced performers and learn the tricks of the "performance of authenticity." Moreover, their usual policy of letting nonunionized singers perform during the afternoon or at the weekly hootenannies provided a time for practice and pushed performers to expand their repertoires. And although some of the lower-end venues had a freak-show atmosphere, exhibiting beatniks, folkniks, and folksingers to Village tourists, it must also be noted that even from a hole-in-the-wall like the Cafe Wha?, singers and co-medians like Dylan, Jimi Hendrix, Richie Havens, Fred Neil, Richard Pryor, and Bill Cosby were able to emerge.

When Dylan came to this scene, he brought a rough per-formance style that had hardly any equal in the clubs of New

York, and which became quickly recognized as a mark of his authenticity. Dylan's style, at the beginning, was largely derivative of Woody Guthrie, and one of the earliest recordings available has him introduced as a singer who "plays around in coffeehouses and sings a lot of songs by Woody Guthrie" ("Hootenannie Special," Riverside Church, WRVR, July 29, 1961). Dylan's fascination with Guthrie gave him a recognizable persona on which to mold his own, and for the first two years in Minneapolis and New York, Dylan was mostly perceived as a Guthrie clone. Even in the imitation of Guthrie, however, one can see some of the features that distinguished Dylan from other performers in the Village. Dylan himself has retrospectively described his early style and repertoire as "more formidable than the rest of the coffeehouse players, my template being hard-core folk songs backed by incessantly loud strumming. I'd either drive people away or they'd come in closer to see what it was all about. There was no in-between" (Dylan 2004b, 17–18). Others have stressed the originality of Dylan's style and his ability to undergo a stylistic metamorphosis every few weeks, "like blotting paper" (as folksinger Liam Clancy told interviewer Patrick Humphries, Bauldie 1992, 50), able to absorb every possible influence from the records and from other performers. Similarly, Dave Van Ronk expressed one of the key aspects of Dylan's appeal, which made him closer to the new generation of urban revivalists, and, therefore, likely to be accepted as part of a crew who valued authenticity. "It was a cultural lag: the boys had discovered Dock Boggs and Mississippi John Hurt, and the girls [like Joan Baez, Judy Collins, and Carolyn Hester] were still listening to Cynthia [Gooding] and Susan Reed.... So whereas the boys were intentionally roughing up their voices, the girls were trying to sound prettier and prettier and more and more virginal" (Van Ronk 2005, 167).

Van Ronk was right; there was a lot of intentionality in Dylan's effort to become "rougher." Early recordings from 1960 bear little resemblance to the familiar Dylan voice of his first record and show a gentler and softer approach that was later to resurface in the country Dylan of *Nashville Skyline*.[6] However, both Dylan and Van Ronk point, quite explicitly, to the relevance of a hard-core aesthetics and its central position as a standard of evaluation in the Village.

To some extent, Dylan had always been on the side of hard-core performers, even when he astonished an audience of high school mates during a badly rehearsed performance of "Rock and Roll Is Here to Stay" in the Hibbing High School auditorium (his principal cut the microphone off, succeeding, where Pete Seeger allegedly failed at Newport). Pursuing a hard-core aesthetics, thus, was quite mandatory in the Village as a means to proclaim authenticity, while at the same time constructing it. Richard Peterson, who has extensively researched the creation of authenticity in country music from its origins to its institutionalization as a genre (Peterson 2005), takes this hard-core aesthetics as one of the poles along a continuum on which singers position themselves. "The basic justification for hard country—Peterson writes —is that it represents the authentic tradition of the music called country and that it is by and for those steeped in the tradition." On the contrary, a soft-shell aesthetics "melds country with pop music to make it enjoyable to the much larger numbers of those not born into or knowledgeable about country music" (Peterson 1997, 150).

Many of the young Dylan's traits made him immediately recognizable as a hard-core performer: the rough voice, the informal speech, the "untrained voice with nasal tone" (Peterson 1997, 151), and most of all the stage presentation. Recollections about Dylan, and the few recordings we have of the 1960–1962 period, hint to the relevance of a hard-core style of expression. It is hard not to picture a twenty-year-old Bob Dylan when we read Peterson's list: the stage presentation of hard-core performer is "informal, friendly, accommodating, modest, including personal anecdotes about self and family; direct connection made with individual audience members, links to hard-core icons" (Peterson 1997, 153).

This hard-core image was established before any serious effort in songwriting on Dylan's part. The expression of authenticity that Dylan pursued on the stage of the Village's coffeehouses and clubs (and other formal or informal venues) was the factor that attracted his peers and secured him a position in Greenwich Village's folk scene. Many recollections, indeed, focus on the peculiarity of Dylan's outfit and performance style and implicitly point to the importance of this hard-core aesthetics in Dylan's early success in the limited circles of the New York scene. The first impression one had of Dylan's style defied the expectations generated by his shabby outfit and young age: "In came this funny-looking kid one night, dressed as if he had just spent a year riding freight trains.... Dylan's early style was a combination of blues, rock, and country which caught on the very minute that he stepped on the stage at Gerde's" (Bauldie 1992, 39). Others pointed to this peculiarity of Dylan's style, which was not one that could be expected from a purist: "He was doing all traditional songs, but it was his approach! His singing style and phrasing were stone rhythm and blues—he fitted the two styles together perfectly" (Bauldie 1992, 38); "And there's this scrawny kid whose voice at first I couldn't stand. It had nothing to do with the criteria that I was used to" (Bauldie 1992, 40). Even for the urban neo-ethnics of the New York scene, Dylan's style and choice of repertoire were probably too eclectic, especially as his voice was finding a distinct sound in the Village coffeehouses, where he often had to strain it in order to make up for the lack of amplification. The better-off, more soft-shell performers usually adopted a totally different vocal style, either a sort of tenor or soprano voice, or they took advantage of the electronic amplification that allowed them to croon. Dylan's hard-core aesthetics moved in the opposite direction, roughing up his voice and offering an act that was not artificially polished, and which soon took advantage of a series of stage routines that he started to perfect in the Village clubs. Many have reported a Chaplinesque persona, with a "flair for comic gesture and the spontaneous quip" and the "rare ability of laughing at himself and at the same time putting across serious material" (Bauldie 1992, 40), and Dylan himself explicitly mentioned Chaplin as a role model, in his usual half-mocking, half-serious tone: "If I'm on stage, my idol—even my biggest idol when I'm on stage—the one that's running through my head all the time, is Charlie Chaplin. And, uh, it, well it takes a while to explain it, but I'd say he's one of 'the' men" (Billy James's unpublished interview for press release of Dylan's first album, 1961).

Still lacking any self-penned material besides a few talking blues (a form of writing that he had directly taken from Woody Guthrie) and the remarkable homage to his idol, "Song to Woody," Dylan had to rely on performance as a means to emerge from the huge cohort of folksingers and create a distinctive sound that met favor with important brokers on the scene, who usually despised soft-shell acts like Harry Belafonte or the Kingston Trio (Bareiss 2010) and the other folk-for-the-masses ensembles that were trying to capitalize on the Trio's success in the late 1950s, creating music that sounded more like "poplore" or manufactured folk (Bluestein 1994). Dylan's positioning on the field of hard-core performers was clear from the very beginning: he had a rough voice, a comic attitude on stage that sounded spontaneous and not "scripted," a distinctive singing style, and a repertoire that was built with reference to other hard-core singers like Woody Guthrie. He even made his debut at Gerde's—one of the important clubs—wearing one of Woody's jackets, given to him by Bob and Sidsel Gleason, a couple of political organizers and folk music enthusiasts who were taking care of Guthrie in New Jersey and who hosted the Sunday meetings where young singers gathered to perform for the ailing Woody.

By September, Dylan had gained the recognition by many of his peers as the new thing in town and was able to get better and better bookings, usually as an opener for more established acts, like John Lee Hooker, The Clancy Brothers, and the Greenbriar Boys. It was while opening for the latter group at Gerde's that he caught the attention of Robert Shelton, folk music critic for the *New York Times,* who wrote a first enthusiastic review of Dylan's performance, focusing on the hard-core features of his stage act:

> A bright new face is appearing at Gerde's Folk City. Although only twenty years old, Bob Dylan is one of the most distinctive stylists to play in a Manhattan cabaret in months. . . .
>
> His clothes may need a bit of tailoring, but when he works his guitar, harmonica or piano and composes new songs faster than he can remember them, there is no doubt that he is bursting at the seams with talent. Mr. Dylan's voice is anything but pretty. He is consciously trying to recapture the rude beauty of a Southern field hand musing in melody on his back porch. All the "husk and bark" are left on his notes, and a searing intensity pervades his songs.
>
> . . . But if not for every taste, his music-making has the mark of originality and inspiration, all the more noteworthy for his youth. Mr. Dylan is vague about his antecedents and birthplace, but it matters less where he has been than where

he is going, and that would seem to be straight up. (Shelton 1961, 31)

Shelton's review has often been perceived as a watershed in Dylan's career, for it meant an extension of his network of supporters, which ultimately led him to the record contract with Columbia records. In other words, Dylan had spent the few months since his arrival in New York gaining recognition from his peers, positioning himself in the hard-core tradition, and producing claims about authenticity that could resonate with that audience.

However, the folk scene had also a particular configuration that in many cases prevented an extension of reputation beyond those circles, what sociologists Gladys and Kurt Lang have identified as the attainment of a wider "renown," which is a fundamental component of artistic reputation (Lang and Lang 2001). Despite the folk scare of the early 1960s, thanks to which folk music was getting more and more attention, the New York scene, and the other scenes in cities and college towns that competed with the Village, still had many of the characteristics of a "restricted field" of production, which French sociologist Pierre Bourdieu (1993) has identified as a field driven by an autonomous logic where—in the case of the folk underground of the Village—music was produced for music's sake, and performers usually had other performers as their primary audience. The folk music scene was governed by a logic of its own, which kept hard-core performers within the safe boundaries created by the scene itself and not completely willing to explore the commercial opportunities opened by the increasing appeal of folk, which were often exploited by more soft-shell performers or even tailor-made ensembles. The hard-core aesthetics was closer to what Bourdieu has identified as a "losers win" logic (Bourdieu 1993, 39), where what is at stake has to do less with economic rewards than with recognition by an intellectually oriented audience (even though the contents of this intellectual orientation are usually defined and negotiated within the scene, without reference to the system of credentials one can find in the outer society); in this context, there was a reversal of commonsense assumptions about fame and success, where new forms of prestige gained more value because they were produced and sanctioned by a network of peers. The recognition of Dylan's authenticity, which was supported by his less-than-formal training, his proclamation of the value of music for music's sake, and his hesitation to accept honors and discomfort in receiving them, was a valuable resource that could be exploited to gain his prominence in the folk music scene. As we shall see, it was a fundamental resource that could be seized in the making of Dylan's reputation as a newcomer with the authority to proclaim a heresy, first by changing the rules of the field in songwriting and second by crossing over to "the masses" by going electric.

Blowin' in the Wind: The Trajectory of a Song and the Extension of Dylan's Network of Supporters

The story of "Blowin' in the Wind," both in and out of the Village, clarifies the dynamics involved in the complex process of the making of Dylan's reputation. "Blowin' in the Wind" was Dylan's first hit, a record that sold more than a million copies in Peter, Paul and Mary's version, and the song that turned things for the better. Although his debut album got excellent reviews, it failed to sell more than five thousand copies (more on this later). Dylan had already caught the attention of many folksingers in the Village with some of his earlier compositions, for example, "The Death of Emmet Till" and "Let Me Die in My Footsteps," but writing "Blowin' in the Wind" was the turning point that accelerated the process of recognition and eventually brought Dylan to national fame. Recognition among his peers and its extension to a broader audience began in the period between the release of his first album in the spring of 1962—when he also wrote "Blowin' in the Wind" and started composing prolifically—and the release of the song in the summer of 1963. This is the period when the prophetic and charismatic narrative about Dylan began, coinciding with the first upturn in his career. For a brief period of time, Dylan wore this prophetic mask, and the folk community reacted enthusiastically, recognizing that Dylan had the potential to become a new folk hero, an image that had always been powerful within the arena of folk music (Rodnitzky 1976).

In late 1961, Dylan already had strong advocates on the scene, and equally strong detractors. Despite its ideology of communalism and collaboration, the folk scene was a competitive one, because resources for singer-songwriters were thin and because the game of authenticity restricted opportunities for hard-core folksingers like Dylan, whose rapid trajectory to the center of the scene, however, put him in touch with the logic of commercialism and the commercial opportunities opened by the folk boom. Thus Dylan, despite all of his efforts to build his own authenticity as a hard-core performer, found himself caught between the restricted field of folk music and a wider system of cultural production. He had the favor of some prominent figures in the circle of hard-core performers, for example, Dave Van Ronk and his wife, Terri, who informally managed him, and Ramblin' Jack Elliot. He also caught the eye of important brokers within the scene, notably Izzy Young, a folk enthusiast who ran the Folklore Center, where members of the folk community hung out, forming and breaking allegiances. Young organized Dylan's first major concert, which was held at the Carnegie Chapter Hall in October 1961. The event turned out to be a flop, attracting only fifty-three paying attendees.

Dylan had also caught the attention of other, less hard-core performers, like Carolyn Hester, for whom he played harmonica at a session for Columbia Records. Through hootenannies and meetings at the Gleasons', he met Pete Seeger, who was never an adversary of folk's commercial opportunities, having witnessed the positive role commercial success could play when he was a member of the Weavers and had chart-topping hits in the late 1940s and early 1950s. More importantly, Dylan had established strong connections with the press—both mainstream newspapers like the *New York Times* and underground papers like *The Village Voice* and the folk fanzine *The Little Sandy Review*, which wrote enthusiastically of his debut album. Dylan also developed an important connection with the powerful record executive and producer John Hammond Sr., who signed him to Columbia and produced his first two albums. Following Hammond's advice, Dylan also signed a management contract with Roy Silver and chose Leeds Music as his publisher. Thus, Dylan's network was a mix of the advocates of hard-core aesthetics he had been acquainted with in the Village and powerful intermediaries who could channel his compositions to a broader audience, either via his own recordings or through other performers who could choose from his catalogue, earning him publishing royalties. This institutional aspect has often gone unnoticed, but the opportunities opened by publishing and having other artists perform his songs probably had some impact on Dylan's transformation from interpreter of songs to songwriter. His productivity exploded in the spring of 1962, and "Blowin' in the Wind" was the turning point that led to the reconfiguration of Dylan's early network, including the addition of new actors.

Dylan admitted that he wrote the song very quickly, in ten or twenty minutes, while sitting in the Fat Black Pussycat, a club on MacDougal Street. If we can believe the apocryphal reconstruction by Dave "Blue" Cohen in Dylan's 1978 movie *Renaldo and Clara,* "[Bob] came over to Gerde's Folk City and played it for Gil Turner, who was scheduled to play that night. Turner thought it was incredible. Bob wrote the words and music down on a sheet of paper, and when Turner went on stage he taped the paper up on the microphone and played the song. Everybody was stunned" (quoted in Heylin 2009, 78). This was probably the second week of April, and Dylan's first known performance of the song followed shortly thereafter, during a stint at Gerde's. This version was still tentative and incomplete, lacking the middle verse, which Dylan added later, possibly at the end of April. He performed the song fairly often in the following months, including a demo for copyright registration and the take for the album *The Freewheelin' Bob Dylan,* which was recorded in July 1962 and released ten months later. By 1964, he had dropped the song from his sets, and it would take ten years and Dylan's comeback tour with The Band in 1974, for it to be regularly included again in his setlists.

To some extent, "Blowin' in the Wind" is still a song rooted in the series of appropriations and transformations that are typical of the folk process. Dylan always acknowledged that the song's antecedent was "No More Auction Block," a spiritual that he had already recorded (and which was later released in *The Bootleg Series vol. 1–3*). There are traces of the spiritual's melody in "Blowin' in the Wind," but there is also a great deal of reworking, as Todd Harvey noted in his remarkable catalogue of the influences of tradition in Dylan's early songs (Harvey 2001, 15). The main innovation, though, regards style, "Blowin' in the Wind" being a departure from the two major genres that Dylan had exploited in his early compositions, the talking blues and the topical song/ballad with a narrative form. "Blowin' in the Wind" is at the same time more universal (like a spiritual) and softer in tone, with the list of questions that set up every verse to end with the statement, "the answer is blowin' in the wind." This is a very ambivalent statement, meaning either that the answer can be found as it blows in the wind or that there is no way to find it, and, therefore, the singer's questions cannot be answered (an ambivalence that Dylan maintains with his stage performances of the song, which take either the form of an optimistic anthem or a sad song of resignation). The very general and universal tone of the lyrics was probably one reason for the controversy surrounding the song in the Village and testifies to Dylan's ambiguous status, even while he was quickly gaining recognition. The song became popular, and many performers started to include it in their sets before it was released or officially recorded. At the same time, it was dismissed by many hard-core performers as "a grocery list song where one line has absolutely no relevance to the next line" (Tom Paxton), dumb (Dave Van Ronk), and "a little easy" (Pete Seeger) (all quoted in Sounes 2001, 114–115).

Thus, the song was received in a peculiar context, where the definition of folk music was constrained by a series of semantic alternatives that shaped the identity of the participants and provided standards for the evaluation of their work. Dylan's "Blowin' in the Wind" defied those basic categories of discourse and interpretation: rural vs. urban, purism vs. innovation, commercialism vs. authenticity, and nonpolitical vs. political or topical. The hard-core circle of the New York scene to which Dylan belonged perceived itself as urban, innovative, authentic, and devoted to political causes. Yet "Blowin' in the Wind" was the product of urban folk, innovative (a song rooted in the folk process but written by a young performer), had a commercial potential, and was only slightly political and certainly not topical. It is surprising, then, that Seeger started to perform it very early on, allegedly by the end of April 1962, and that the song was published for the first time on the cover of *Broadside*, a fanzine focused on topical songwriting, which Seeger strongly supported and where Dylan served on the editorial board (though he was later to dismiss his contribution as a career move).

Writing "Blowin' in the Wind" probably accelerated other changes in Dylan's network of supporters, not only within the circle of performers and Village representatives, but among those crucial entrepreneurs who could boost Dylan's fame beyond the folk scene. In August 1962, Albert Grossman replaced Roy Silver as Dylan's manager, and he urged Dylan to choose Witmark and Sons as his publishing company, under a deal that offered Grossman huge benefits. Grossman, as a business shark and a tough manager, was openly despised in the folk scene, especially by the heralds of authenticity and political commitment who made up a large contingent in New York. However, he also saw very early on the commercial potential of Dylan's songwriting, which blossomed in 1962. Grossman already managed other acts, like Odetta and most importantly, Peter, Paul, and Mary, a manufactured folk trio that was crossing over to mainstream audiences while retaining important traits of "political" authenticity that merged seamlessly with their soft-shell sound and image. Grossman was thus able to exploit the opportunities of having under his wing a hard-core performer with remarkable songwriting skills and a more soft-shell act who had an interest (it is not clear whether it was also an economic interest) in building a strong repertoire that went beyond traditional songs. Peter, Paul, and Mary's hit in 1962 had been a pop-folk version of Seeger's "If I Had a Hammer," which reached the top ten, while their debut album spent seven weeks at number one and sold two million copies. The formula was successful: a catchy song, written by a performer attuned to the folk sensibility, which had a general political content (the keywords in "If I Had a Hammer" are *justice* and *freedom*), sweetened by the trio's well-crafted harmonies and spiced up by Mary Travers's sensual presence. Peter, Paul, and Mary's hit of 1963 was "Blowin' in the Wind," after it received pretty much the same treatment.

We see here the dynamics at work in Dylan's early success, which created controversy for his association with pop acts and which—nonetheless—was able to affect in a positive way his transition from urban revivalist with a repertoire of old blues and country traditionals to respected singer-songwriter. The accomplishment of this transition meant Dylan's first touch of fame and his dismissal of an early persona in favor of a new image that focused on his role as a "poet," and a songwriter who could create songs that other performers were eager to cover and adapt for larger audiences. During this period, however, Dylan was still a maverick on the scene, at least until the national break of "Blowin' in the Wind." In the song's trajectory, we see interactions and appropriations that involved two different sectors of the folk revival that were competing for recognition in the national arena: The first was the circle of hard-core performers on the New York scene and their politically oriented allies, who framed "Blowin' in the Wind" as a departure from the earlier image of authenticity that Dylan had pursued successfully since his arrival in New York. The second sector was a larger network that was willing to support Dylan and which was more deeply embedded in the music and entertainment industry, with access to more resources and relations than the network of left-leaning impresarios, jazz and folk record labels, and small publishers that were usually active in the folk revival. The network included major labels like Columbia and Warner, whose executives were professional managers, who not only had a roster of acts that could support each other, but also were strategically positioned in the hard-core and soft-shell camps, and traditional publishing companies that had a financial interest in the circulation of songs.

For Dylan, though, the problem remained pretty much the same. His songs were crossing over successfully, thanks to their appropriation by more popular singers, with clean voices and a less idiosyncratic style of guitar playing. This meant that for the hard-core Dylan it was still difficult to reach other audiences, already accustomed to the folk-for-the-masses products of the early 1960s. By the time he released his second album, which was met with a higher commercial success than *Bob Dylan*, he was already involved in an attempt to bring his hard-core authenticity to larger masses, a trait that was one of the more enduring of his career trajectory. His brief phase as a topical songwriter and perceived "prophet" of the civil rights movement and his generation was a first step in this process.

Dylan's Ambivalent Reputation in the Folk Revival

In 1963, Pete Seeger and Joan Baez were the dean and the queen of the folk revival. Revivalists still lacked a king though, one to follow in Baez's and Seeger's footsteps. The two established artists had clear ideas about their candidate for the crown. Their 1963 recordings are filled with Dylan-penned songs, ranging from "Blowin' in the Wind" to "Who Killed Davey Moore," from "A Hard Rain's A-Gonna Fall" to "Don't Think Twice It's Alright." Odetta; Peter, Paul, and Mary; the Chad Mitchell Trio; Judy Collins; The Kingston Trio; and many others followed suit. Dylan provided them quality songwriting in a field where songs were a scarce resource, and performers had two main strategies to build their own, recognizable repertoire: they could rely on old recordings of traditional or quasi-traditional material, with the risk of being labeled neo-ethnics and purists, or they could focus on topical songwriting, leaning more toward the political side of the folk revival. Dylan was able to offer a blend of these two categories, both by adapting old songs for new compositions and by offering a new approach to topical songs that was less focused on the news and more on universalistic concerns. Fellow performers became strong supporters of Dylan's reputation, introducing his songs during their sets like others had done in the Village, the only difference being, everything happened at a different level.

In just a few months, *The Freewheelin' Bob Dylan* climbed to number twenty-two in Billboard's charts; Dylan was booked to play on *The Ed Sullivan Show* but stormed out of the theater after his satire of American anti-communists ("Talking John Birch Society Blues") was rejected by CBS's censors; he flew down to Mississippi, the land of the blues, with Pete Seeger and Theo Bikel and played during a registration rally; he became a star at the Newport Folk Festival in July; he sang at the March on Washington; and was booed off stage when he delivered the acceptance speech at the Tom Paine Award ceremony. In the wake of President Kennedy's assassination, saying that he could see something of himself in Lee Harvey Oswald was probably a bit too much. In other words, 1963 was the year of commitment.

It was also the year of performing. Dylan played at Newport, in Washington, shared the bill with Joan Baez on a short tour that sold out quickly, and finally made it to the Carnegie Hall. With performance and exposure came image trouble, when "Bob Dylan," Robert Zimmerman's creation, was suddenly exposed in public by a profile *Newsweek* published the week Dylan played at the Carnegie Hall. The profile challenged Dylan, revealing his middle-class background and the fact that his parents were in the audience at the Carnegie Hall, as well as inaugurating the legend that he didn't write "Blowin' in the Wind," rather, had purchased it from a New Jersey student, Lorre Wyatt—a rumor that was patently false but which circulated even after Wyatt recanted.

More interesting is the threat on authenticity that was posed by the *Newsweek* article:

> Why Dylan—he picked the name in admiration for Dylan Thomas—should bother to deny his past is a mystery. Perhaps he feels it would spoil the image he works so hard to cultivate—with his dress, with his talk, with the deliberately atrocious grammar and pronunciation in his songs. He says he hates the commercial side of folk music, but he has two agents who hover about him, guarding his words and fattening his contracts. He scorns the press's interest in him, but he wants to know how long a story about him will run and if there will be a photograph. He is a complicated young man, surrounded now by complicated rumors. (Svedburg 1963, 95)

Vicious as it was (and certainly as it was perceived by Dylan, who retaliated with bitter remarks in "Restless Farewell," one of the songs he recorded for *The Times They Are A-Changin'*), *Newsweek*'s article revealed the ongoing tension in Dylan's career and in the folk revival in general. How can authenticity be performed when audiences see authenticity itself as a valuable product in an industrialized system of production? The polarization between authenticity (raw, hard-core) and commercialism had constituted a major point of debate since folk had found new popularity. Writing in 1964, Irwin Silber (always a watchdog of the scene and editor of *Sing Out!*) stressed that "many of the worst aspects of the rat-race culture have become significant influences on our folk-music tradition." Again, it was the politicized vision of tradition that Silber pushed for, fearing that the cult of authenticity could be suffocated by the emergence of a retreatist "cult of tradition" per se: "Others, in rejecting the 'commercial,' have helped develop the 'cult of tradition' —disavowing the possibilities of our age finding its own expression," tradition becoming "an end in itself" (Silber 1964, in DeTurk and Poulin 1967, 301). Along with him, many others feared a watered-down, commercial version of folk, exactly at the same time revivalists were creating a strong connection with the struggles of the civil rights movement. In this context, what the editors of the *Little Sandy Review* (Paul Nelson and Jon Pancake, two advocates of the cult of tradition Silber was shooting down) had typecast as "the protesty people" were able to offer a political vision of authenticity that swept away many of the connotations that had accompanied the earlier, neo-ethnic aspirations of urban revivalists. Authenticity had to be topical; otherwise it was not authentic at all.

Dylan's image as the "prophet of protest" settled in this context, although very early on, he had been extremely wary of the implications a close association with just topical songwriting could foster, proclaiming that he would "stand behind" the topical songs he had written, but that he also wanted to "write from the inside of me," as some of the songs he included in his most topical albums showed. These cautions notwithstanding, Dylan fit the ideal of a new generation of topical songwriters, elevated to the status of poets, who could take the torch from their Old-Left, Popular Front–influenced mentors. For a year, and until the English tour of the spring of 1965, Dylan opened his concerts with his anthem "The Times They Are A-Changin'," a song whose composition he later remembered as an attempt to write "a song with a purpose" (as he told Cameron Crowe in the booklet notes for his retrospective box set *Biograph,* released in 1985), crafted with the goal of seizing the spirit of the times. "The Times They Are A-Changin'," and other songs—"When the Ship Comes In," "Masters of War," even the lesser-known "Paths of Victory"—were exhortations performed with a prophetic tone and carried an optimism that meant that the times indeed they were a-changing. At the same time, Dylan wrote in the apocalyptic tradition and in invectives that portrayed the world as having no shades of gray.

Stephen Scobie is one of the scholars who has explored Dylan's mask as a prophet more deeply, offering a charismatic view of the artist that seemed to fit the Dylan who was on his road to stardom well: political, even topical, prophetic—an image that has stuck with the public and that has influenced the reception of Dylan's work for years. Like other prophets and social disruptors in general, Dylan builds his strength on his ability to break rules and create new ones almost from scratch. The prophetic model seems to fit Dylan, because a prophet is a "highly individualized figure," who derives "his authority not from any institution, but from the assertion of his personal vocation" (Scobie 2003, 26). However, individualism challenged the communitarian premises on which the folk revival established its legitimacy as a "purer" and "noncontaminated" arena within American culture. Dylan's vision in these crucial years (which Scobie has identified with "the years of creation," and which I contend are also the years of the creation of one among many "Bob Dylans") was consistent with the presence of "a strong element of prophetic stance: a sternly moralizing view of the world, a keen eye for social injustice and suffering, a demand for America to live up to its Puritan self-conception" (Scobie 2003, 30). Yet it must also be noted that the prophet—like its ironic alter ego, the trickster—lives up to the promise delivered by his prophecy only when the latter is projected toward an audience. Charisma, as sociologists often say, is less a matter of natural, objective qualities and more a matter of recognition by faithful followers. The prophet, thus, is always trapped in the cage he has created by breaking the rules and by establishing the exception of his own rule. He needs to be reminded constantly that people believe in him, lest he lose his power to create the illusion of his exceptionality.

Dylan the prophet, the next-to-last incarnation of the folk Dylan, or the pre-rock Dylan, saw very early on that the prophetic mask was a cage: "I ain't no prophet, and I ain't no prophet's son" ("Long Time Gone," 1963, Witmark Demo). And he dismissed the myth of protest even while he was creating it. Yet, Dylan's topical period, which peaked in 1963, developed within the tensions created by his increasing commercial appeal, the demands from different parties that pressured him to become even more political, and his repositioning from urban revivalist who had come to New York looking for neither love nor money, but singers, to rising star. These changes cast doubts among his supporters, doubts that were voiced once again by Irwin Silber in an open letter that reacted to the metamorphosis of the former protégé of the folk revival:

You seem to be in a different kind of bag now, Bob—and I'm worried about it. I saw at Newport how you had somehow lost contact with people. It seemed to me that some of the paraphernalia of fame were getting in your way. You travel with an entourage now—with good buddies who are going to laugh when you need laughing and drink wine with you and insure your privacy—and never challenge you to face everyone else's reality again....

You said you weren't a writer of "protest" songs—or any other category, for that matter—but you just wrote songs. Well, okay, call it anything you want. But any songwriter who tries to deal honestly with reality in this world is bound to write "protest" songs. How can he help himself?

Your new songs seem to be all inner-directed now, innerprobing, self-conscious—maybe even a little maudlin or a little cruel on occasion. And it's happening on stage, too. You seem to be relating to a handful of cronies behind the scenes now—rather than to the rest of us out front. (Silber 1964, in McGregor 1990, 66–68)

Usually, critics pick up Silber's remarks in order to discuss the changes in Dylan's songs, which were expanding on the symbolist references he had already put to test in "A Hard Rain's A-Gonna Fall." They take one of Silber's casual comments—"it's happening on stage, too"—as relatively unimportant, but one of the keys to understanding Dylan's metamorphosis from the working-class wannabe who's on the cover of *The Times They Are A-Changin'* to the hipster who appears in the opening sequence of D. A. Pennebaker's cinéma-vérité documentary *Dont Look Back,* is indeed performance. Not only because performance made the struggles between these two Dylans visible, but also because it was an occasion to entertain a dialogue with—or to warn, for that matter—his audience. In his booklet notes to the *Bootleg Series vol. 6,* documenting the Halloween 1964 concert at the Philharmonic Hall, historian Sean Wilentz—who attended the concert—wrote of an audience that left the hall "exhilarated, entertained, and ratified in our self-assured enlightenment, but also confused about the snatches of lines we'd gleaned from the strange new songs" (now in Wilentz 2010, 91). Wilentz recalls his sense of estrangement upon hearing for the first time "Gates of Eden" and "It's Alright Ma (I'm Only Bleeding)," but focuses little on one of the throwaways of the night, "If You Gotta Go, Go Now," trapped between the two anthems that were going to make half of the astounding second side of *Bringing It All Back Home.* "If You Gotta Go, Go Now" is a transitional song like "Mr. Tambourine Man," or "Chimes of Freedom," only in a different way. It is a song that at the Philharmonic receives the *Another Side of Bob Dylan* treatment, meaning a song that goes so naturally toward rock and roll (Manfred Mann was to have a hit in the United Kingdom with an electric arrangement similar to the one Dylan used) that any acoustic version inevitably sounds like an unfinished demo.

The performance at the Philharmonic is important because it reveals for Dylan a direction that all those who were criticizing (or praising) him had not yet foreseen. Despite its comic tone (people were laughing at the Philharmonic Hall), "If You Gotta Go, Go Now" was a song that Dylan decided to carry with him throughout his English tour of 1965, and he even attempted to record it with electronic backing twice, during the *Bringing It All Back Home* sessions and, later in May, at the end of the British tour, with John Mayall and the Heartbreakers. "If You Gotta Go, Go Now" departs more radically from the clichés about Dylan that had circulated within the folk revival than other songs that Silber and others were criticizing. It is simultaneously nontopical, nontraditional, and nonpoetic, with its comic lines about sex and hooking up that were very explicit. Whereas "It's Alright Ma" was an ultimate protest that Dylan sarcastically introduced at the Philharmonic Hall as "a very funny song," only to stun the audience, "If You Gotta Go, Go Now" was adult pop with irony, and Dylan started singing it for what it was, a project for a rock and roll single, for people who wanted to go beyond the teenage naïveté of "I Want to Hold Your Hand."

Dylan's response to the critiques of important entrepreneurs who thought they interpreted the feelings of his audience was just a few months down the road. Whereas in Newport 1964 he had challenged his critics with slim-fit trousers, Wayfarer sunglasses, and two inner-directed songs ("It Ain't Me, Babe" and "Mr. Tambourine Man"), by 1965 he was ready to add to his "handful of cronies" a few musicians who could play some loud, electric rock and roll. This transition created a breach in the folk revival and ultimately led to its demise as an important musical force in the United States.

Performance played a central role in it, starting with Dylan's much talked about appearance at the Newport Folk Festival and ending with the motorcycle accident that, in July 1966, put an end to the most frantic and one of the most creative phases of Dylan's career.

Notes

1. The quotations are, respectively, from "Mississippi," "Tweedle Dee and Tweedle Dum," and "High Water (For Charley Patton)." On the reception of "*Love and Theft*" in the wake of 9/11, see especially Farley (2001), Gilmore (2001), Gundersen (2001), Hilburn (2001), and Wilentz (2003).

2. Unless otherwise noted, all Dylan's comments during the shows have been transcribed by the author, and cross-checked with already available transcriptions, especially those published in Olof Bjoerner's tour guides (www.bjoerner.com/bob.htm), whom I thank for his permission to use the files he has compiled for my research.

3. The relationship between Dylan and the Midwest, his youth, and the influence of Hibbing on his work has attracted the attention of writers and critics since the early 1960s. One of the best among early accounts is still Thompson's *Positively Main Street* (Thompson 2008). In his biography, Robert Shelton conducted extensive research and had access to Dylan's family (Shelton 1986, 21–62; Shelton 2004, 15–36). Pichaske (2010) argues in favor of the centrality of a "Midwest framework" to understand Dylan's work, and to date it is the most informed, if not always convincing, scholarly take on this subject. See also Clayton (2009). Recently, the theme of space and place has become an interesting, and still relatively unexplored, small subfield in the critical literature on Dylan; see Child (2009), Elliott (2009), and Smart (2009).

4. This constructionist perspective does not deny that *perceived genius* can have powerful consequences both on audiences and artists themselves, pressured to act and produce art in accordance with that narrative (and indeed these pressures have played a huge role in Dylan's definition of his own art, as well as in his attempt to escape from the label of genius). It argues, however, that any attempt to see the artist as the one and only source of his greatness, ignoring the system of relations and interactions in which he works, leads to a naturalistic fallacy. Probably the most compelling sociological study of this dynamic and relational approach is DeNora's work on Beethoven (1995). For a general statement of the problem, see DeNora and Mehan (1993).

5. Dylan himself has played, recorded, and performed many songs that were originally published in Smith's anthology, and it has long been rumored that a hard-to-find copy was among the records Dylan stole from the Minneapolis apartment of his friend Jon Pancake. However, he has also dismissed more recent public claims about its centrality in the folk revival: "All those people—you could hear the actual people singing those ballads. You could hear Clarence Ashley, Doc Watson, Dock Boggs, The Memphis Jug Band, Furry Lewis. You could see those people live and in person. They were around. Performers did know of that record, but it wasn't, in retrospect, the monumental iconic recordings at the time" (Gilmore 2001a, 66). For an account of the trajectory of the *Anthology* from commercial failure to founding document of American vernacular music, see Skinner (2006).

6. Early tapes from 1960 and 1961, recorded either in New York or in the Twin Cities, show indeed a softer tone in Dylan's voice, to the point that its authenticity has sometimes been questioned, like in the case of the so-called Karen Wallace Tape (which has partially leaked to collectors). On these early documents of Dylan's maturation, see especially Heylin (1995, 2–6).

Two

There's No Success Like Failure

Performance and Audience Mobilization in the Electric Turn

Playing rock and roll at the Newport Folk Festival was not outrageous in 2002. After all, Dylan had already shocked Newport in 1965, and everything he was planning for his comeback after thirty-seven years would have certainly paled by comparison. It turned out that he had not planned anything special, or maybe considering Newport 2002 just another show in the long saga of his Never Ending Tour was itself something to be talked about. Yet, he was able to get the ghost of electricity back for a brief moment. It happened during the encores, when Dylan and his band ventured into the opening chords of Buddy Holly's last great song, "Not Fade Away," a song that is the epitome of pre-bubblegum rock and roll, a phase that ended symbolically when Holly died in a plane crash on February 3, 1959. Nearly forty years later, when Dylan received three Grammy awards for his acclaimed *Time Out of Mind* (1997), Holly was still a haunting presence:

> I just want to say that when I was sixteen or seventeen years old, I went to see Buddy Holly play at Duluth National Guard Armory and I was three feet away from him . . . and he looked at me. And I just have some sort of feeling that he was—I don't know how or why—but I know he was with us all the time we were making this record in some kind of way.

"Not Fade Away" soon entered the setlists, and for a few years it was the standard encore of Dylan's shows. At Newport it was a familiar explosion of garage sound, with Dylan supported on backing vocals by guitarists Charlie Sexton and Larry Campbell. There was no sacrilege, because Holly had already become an American icon and early rock and roll a part of tradition, a sign that tradition always changes.

It was much more adventurous to go electric in 1965. In this chapter, I will analyze Dylan's most controversial transition, from folk to rock, and I will try to understand how Dylan's reputation and artist-image were reconfigured in the course of this highly contentious process. I will argue that understanding the "electric turn" makes little sense if we do not consider how Dylan performed it in public as a way to reposition himself in the field of popular music, while being simultaneously involved as one of the protagonists of a debate about "Dylan going electric" and "selling out" that implied work on the social meanings of the artist and his art. Performances were the setting for the creation of Dylan's total image as a mid-1960s icon, and starting in Newport, they catalyzed into an "event" (what came to be perceived as Dylan's "electric turn") a series of interconnected incidents, confrontations, public appearances, and discourses produced in and around the presentation of the New Dylan. When these local occurrences are linked in a narrative and reproduced for wider audiences, they acquire an "iconic" status that is further used to symbolize more general processes of cultural change. If we focus on the specific case of the whole controversy that surrounded Dylan in 1965–1966, the emergence of this new structure of meanings had wider effects, because it led to the transformation of the institutional field of folk music, the emergence of the rock musician as a symbolic figure (as opposed to both the folksinger and the pop artist), and the creation of a new public that, alongside Dylan, aligned itself with the emerging values of rock.

The electric turn, or so the myth goes, was everything but a smooth transition. It involved the production of a completely new rhetoric of authenticity that had to be communicated to a fragmented audience. It was on the relationship between the actor and the audience that the success of performance depended in the final instance. When he had to face the audience, however, Dylan's claims about his newly found authenticity became much more vulnerable, especially because audiences are always selective when it comes to define what the artist "means" to them from the affective and cognitive point of view, namely, the image members of the audience hold of an artist and the feelings that are attached to this image.

In the following pages, I will focus on the characteristics of this interpretive conflict and analyze how Dylan (and the coalition of his supporters) was able to establish his new image as a pioneer of popular culture, when he initially had to face a nearly total disaffiliation from his reference audience.

Newport, July 25, 1965: The Original Breach

Dylan's electric set at Newport has become a landmark moment in the history of popular music, to the extent that it is very difficult to separate the performance (roughly forty minutes, five songs) from the myth that began to be passed around minutes after Dylan walked off the stage. It has become so charged with meaning that—as Lee Marshall has argued—"it is used to symbolize the closing of one chapter and the opening of another, both in terms of Dylan's own career and with regards to popular music as a whole" (Marshall 2007, 89; see also Marshall 2006). Dylan's appearance at the Newport Folk Festival, however, should not be seen as a sudden turning point, but rather as a moment of contention over all the tensions that had strained the folk revival for at least two years, and which became further polarized in the aftermath of the show. It was, in anthropologist Victor Turner's words, a point in a complex "social drama" (Turner 1974, 1982), where actors performed their mutual opposition and aligned to old or emerging values that were competing for recognition, a conflict made visible through a highly symbolic moment of breach of established expectations both in performative and normative terms. Greil Marcus has written, on a similar if less analytic vein, of a shocking performance that "forced people to take sides" (Marcus 2005, 159) and to signal where they stood in the big "selling out" controversy, as fierce supporters or as detractors and—with a reasonable amount of hindsight—as villains.

Contentious moments like these never come unannounced, but are preceded by a progressive strain in personal and social relations (within society at large or within more sharply defined subsectors or fields) and by a challenge to the values that underlie the everyday life of a group or community. The folk revival had indeed changed considerably since 1964, but Dylan's appearance at Newport drew the public attention to a whole different level, because there was an "event" that expressed under public scrutiny the contradictions that the folk revival was trying to resolve. The identities of both the artist and the folk revival at large were questioned, as well as Dylan's own positioning in this context, because he had switched over a short time span from urban traditionalist, to protest singer, to poet—as Peter Yarrow, who was emceeing at Newport, implicitly acknowledged when he called Dylan on stage:

> Coming up now, is a person who in a sense has changed the face of folk music to the large American public, because he has brought to it a point of view of a poet. Ladies and gentlemen, the person that's gonna come up now has a limited amount of time [puzzlement within the audience, Yarrow speaks with a slightly stressed voice]. His name is Bob Dylan.

Up to that point, "poetry" had been a major frame at work in the classification of Dylan as both an intellectual and a popular artist, even though for every Pete Seeger, who publicly praised Dylan's talents, there was always a very critical Ewan MacColl, who eloquently dismissed Dylan's work as the efforts of "a youth of mediocre talent," full of "cultivated illiteracy" and "embarrassing fourth-grade schoolboy attempts at free verse" (MacColl, Ochs, et al. 1967). Dylan's status as a poet, who could embody the romance of the outsider and establish a "poetry" that spoke of and for authenticity, had been produced, recognized, and questioned mostly within the boundaries of that particular cultural milieu. It, therefore, bore an association to music that could not bypass the constraints imposed on the performance of lyrics-as-poetry and that featured acoustic music as a powerful—and almost the only acceptable—means of expression. This feeling was seemingly reinforced by the very different status and aesthetic complexity of the electric and the semi-acoustic side of *Bringing It All Back Home,* Dylan's latest album; the electric tracks were witty blues, sarcastic rock and roll, reminiscent of Dylan's talking blues, or lyrics that expanded the inner-directedness of *Another Side of Bob Dylan,* whereas on the acoustic side, Dylan's symbolism reached its climax and an unsurpassed coherence. This opposition, which was not yet a difference of values but rather a perceived difference of style, found its way at Newport in the semantic and performative opposition that marked "Maggie's Farm" during the electric set and "It's All Over Now Baby Blue" and "Mr. Tambourine Man" in the short, afterthought-like acoustic encore.

It was quite clear, as soon as Dylan appeared on Newport's stage, that he was not alone. He had rehearsed his electric set during the afternoon (evidence that debunks the myth that his choice to go electric was totally unexpected), and musicians as well as instruments were visible on the stage. There is a guitar tuning somewhere (Mike Bloomfield), some organ chords try to find their way (Al Kooper), a piano riff, a snare drum. Then, Dylan starts strumming his Fender Stratocaster. The band hopes to find a groove, given the little time they had to rehearse. Then Dylan (or was it Bloomfield?), probably turning to the rhythm section, shouts "Let's go!" and a punk version of "Maggie's Farm" thunders through the night, with its complaint about people wanting "you to be just like them."

"Maggie's Farm" seemed an apt choice, but the outcome of that shocking five-minute performance was a total shipwreck of meanings, as Dylan both challenged and defeated the expectations of his audience. Typically for Dylan, the song has the ambiguous lyrics that can refer simultaneously to a condition of society (hence the easy interpretation of "Maggie's Farm" as a kind of protest song by some folk revivalists), his audience, and all those who were putting excessive pressures on him. For its tone and possible topic, the song was attuned to the sensibility of the Newport crowd. It is not surprising that Pete Seeger often tried to justify his rage at Newport as a consequence of the bad music Dylan was performing and the volume at which it was played and not as a result of his contrariety to rock and electric music as a means to carry a politically progressive message.

I couldn't understand the words. I wanted to hear the words. It was a great song, "Maggie's Farm," and the sound was distorted. I ran over to the guy at the controls and shouted, "Fix the sound so you can hear the words." He hollered back, "This is the way they want it." I said "Damn it, if I had an axe, I'd cut the cable right now." (Kupfer 2001)

Seeger's remark is valuable, because it highlights at least some of the issues that were at stake during Dylan's performance, not least the prominence of the "message" as opposed to the sound, and therefore of Dylan's status as a "spokesman" as opposed to performer and musician. Nor was Seeger alone in voicing his dissatisfaction with the sound. Dylan himself, when he recalled the event a few weeks later in an interview with Nora Ephron and Susan Edmiston, complained that the main problem at Newport was that "they twisted the sound on me before I began," hardly a possibility, because the public address system was well guarded by Dylan's acolytes (Cott 2006, 52).

The challenge of the three-song electric set concerned simultaneously the background representations, the scripts of performance, the claim to the legitimate use of social and symbolic power, as well as the concrete arrangement of the mise-en-scène and the means of symbolic production, what sociologist Jeffrey Alexander has identified as the key elements of a social performance that have to be connected in order to project an impression of authenticity that "fuses" actors and audiences together as a collective (Alexander 2004). The reputation of Dylan as an artist in transition regarded all those aspects of the performance, and it was through the conscious manipulation of material and symbolic elements that he attempted to reshape his self-image for his audience. Other artists, on the contrary, would not challenge those external expectations about authenticity, either because they had actively created them (like Pete Seeger), or because their status could have been damaged by the adoption of a different configuration of elements (something that Dylan had done and that, for example, Richard Fariña, who had considered playing electric at Newport, could not use to his advantage: Hajdu 2001).

With the electric set, Dylan positioned himself outside the aesthetic standards of the folk revival, both visually and sonically. The Dylan who played electric at Newport had dismissed the egalitarian and proletarian apparel he had worn in his folk years, and adopted a hipper image. He was wearing a polka dot shirt during the afternoon rehearsal, and for the night concert he appeared with a bright orange shirt, a leather jacket, and Beatle boots. Nothing could have been more different than the aesthetics of simplicity that the revivalists evoked. In the performance at the Newport Folk Festival, every aspect of Dylan's image defied expectations, creating an inconsistency in his image for a relevant sector of his audience, which in turn counter-projected another vision that had been shaped in the previous years and that marked some relevant aspects of Dylan within the frame of a political-aesthetic configuration of sound and values.[1]

Nor did the end of the concert make things any more normal. Dylan was expected to play for forty-five minutes, but after just three songs, he shouted another "Let's go men! That's all!" and left the stage. Accounts of the event often claim that the crowd's uproar was because of Dylan's extremely short set, although when one listens to the break between "Like a Rolling Stone" and "Phantom Engineer," it's apparent that the audience was protesting even in the middle of the electric set. After the last song ended, the crowd starts yelling so loud the roar smothers Yarrow's difficult attempt to negotiate Dylan's return to the stage. Cries of "we want Dylan!" mixed with boos and cheers, go on for several minutes, and Yarrow has to assure the audience that Dylan will be coming back with an acoustic guitar (probably lent to him either by Yarrow or, as the myth-within-the-myth goes, by a very supportive Johnny Cash). "He's gonna get his ax … an acoustic guitar," Yarrow says. Dylan is heard in the background asking for another guitar, as if for the first time he has lost control of his trademark instrument, something that would also happen when he asked for an E harmonica and several harps were thrown on the stage (a trick to connect the artist and the audience in a sort of performative complicity that he had probably learned during the days in the Village and that he used again at the Hollywood Bowl). The second part of Dylan's performance is as charged with meanings as the opening electric set. He tunes the guitar, blows a few notes on the harmonica, starts strumming, asks again for another guitar, hopefully he is given one, somebody shouts something from the crowd, the response is laughter from other sectors of the audience, Dylan seems lost. Then, slowly, a harp introduction leads into "It's All Over Now Baby Blue."

Compared with the punk sound of the electric set, it is at the same time a tired and a fascinating performance. Was it a warning to the audience, or simply the performance of a song that Dylan has always been quite proud of? Certainly, the line about "the lover who has just walked out the door" made more sense at Newport than in any of the other venues Dylan has performed the song before or since. But what mattered to the audience was probably that Dylan had backed down and met their expectations. If the first half of the concert had been met with silence and booing, the acoustic set was characterized by another type of silence, one fully consistent with the scripts that regulated the performance of acoustic songs. The audience applauded immediately after the first line, then roared with applause at the end of the song, which lasted an interminable amount of time, until Dylan started —or pretended to start—"Mr. Tambourine Man."

A short, telltale fragment ensues, with Dylan strumming the chords of "Mr. Tambourine Man," then saying with a weary voice, "Alright, I'll do this one." Then he asks for the harmonica that eventually lands on the stage. When he reaches the first request for the "Tambourine Man" to play a song, a few women scream. A total reversal of Beatlemania, when only the artist alone on stage (and not a group playing electric instruments) can cause such polite hysteria, in a community where stardom and celebrity were evidence of "selling out" to the music industry.[2]

At Newport, the complex dynamic of audience affiliation and disaffiliation went full circle in the short time it took to perform five songs. Puzzlement, anger, and relief seem to have dominated the set, and indeed this emotional aspect was central to the local interpretation of the event. These feelings and emotions were embedded in and acted out in the performance, something that Dylan did not probably foresee before he went on stage. However, the style and the aesthetic choice that Dylan embodied on stage caused a sudden fragmentation of his audience. The folk audience's disenchantment with Dylan took the shape of a local confrontation with the quality of the performance and with the political values it articulated. To become the controversial event it has become—one of the most crucial episodes in the history of popular music—the audience (and to some extent Dylan himself) had to engage in a struggle to extend the local meanings of the performance to a wider context of debate. Here, Dylan proved to have the resources and a coalition of supporters that was able to make his actions acquire a new meaning, that Newport opened a new path for popular music. However, this struggle over symbols and the meaning of the performance was not an easy one, especially if we consider the aftermath of Newport and the attacks on Dylan's reputation, which now became increasingly contested.

Polarization and the Big Folk-Rock Debate

Dylan's appearance at Newport suddenly challenged the boundaries that the folk scene had drawn in the preceding years: as Theodore Bikel remarked after Newport, "you do not whistle in church; you don't play rock 'n' roll at a folk festival" (Mirken 1965, 13).[3] The booing, the catcalls, and the demand to play acoustic, which pressured Dylan into backing down temporarily, were all symbolic practices aimed at the preservation of what the folk revivalists had constructed over the years to separate their scene from mainstream American society and culture. Boundary work, as sociologist Paul DiMaggio argues, is in fact "highly ritualized" (DiMaggio 1987), because it requires a collective intervention on symbols, narratives, and actions that is pursued collectively and that involves the making of musical and artistic genres as patterns that mix together aesthetic principles, orientations to the interpretation of artistic work, and criteria for the evaluation of the position of an artist within or outside the artistic space defined by the boundary (Appelrouth 2011).

The boundaries built by active members of the folk scene were, as I have argued, both political and aesthetic, but they had started to be challenged in a number of ways even before Dylan made the challenge public at Newport. Their erosion came, indeed, from different sectors of the field of cultural production. The Beatles' debut on the *Ed Sullivan Show* and the British Invasion that followed starting in early 1964 is usually regarded as one of the factors that changed the landscape. Here comes a quartet of long-haired guys from Liverpool, England, raised on a diet of skiffle and early rock and roll, who are able to talk to the ghosts of Buddy Holly and Eddie Cochran. In their own way, the Beatles, too, were "authentic," or were able to project an image of authenticity that was embedded in a different sector of cultural production; they had been influenced, after all, by "authentic" rock and roll and by the sounds of Motown and girl groups that came from a racial periphery, and had little to share with the bubblegum music that characterized the tailor-made products for teenagers of the early 1960s.

The impact of the sudden transformation led by the Beatles and other British Invasion groups on the new generation of folksingers—who had flirted with rock and roll in their teens—was enormous.[4] Dylan recalled a road trip to New Orleans and California, where he and his pals "were driving through Colorado, we had the radio on, and eight of the top-10 songs were Beatles songs.... They were doing things that nobody was doing.... I knew they were pointing the direction of where music had to go" (Scaduto, 1971, 203–204). Up to that point, pop music and rock and roll had been a kind of guilty pleasure for the young folkies, listened to in hiding or talked about with conspiratorial caution, as both Carolyn Hester (who had been briefly associated with Buddy Holly) and Richard Fariña recalled of their meetings with Dylan (Hajdu 2001). To many others, however, rock and roll (or better, "popular" and "commercial" music) meant a different world, far away from the perceived, and self-constructed, purity of the folk scene, even though some years before, Alan Lomax (who would eventually play the part of the villain in the controversy over the electric turn) had praised the new music and even featured a versatile rock and roll and doo-wop group (The Cadillacs) in the Folksong '59 concert he organized at Carnegie Hall (Cohen 2002, 139–140).

These early attempts at musical integration notwithstanding, the meaning of rock and roll changed slowly, and by the mid-1960s the folk revival had resumed its negative attitude toward commercialism, both with regard to the internal boundaries of the scene (hard-core vs. soft-shell performers) and within the broader system of the cultural industry. Usually, broader renown and fame were potential markers of stigma. Such was the fate of many professional, semiprofessional, or "commercial" folk artists, from the Kingston Trio, to Peter, Paul, and Mary, to other market-oriented folk acts in the heyday of the revival. Characterized by a high degree of professionalism, this milieu was where the original folk-rockers came from. If we look at the trajectory within the folk scene of the artists to whom the label "folk-rock" was attached, we witness indeed an origin in the ideological and cultural periphery of the revival. Roger McGuinn, David Crosby, and Gene Clark (founding members of The Byrds, the main protagonist of the American "reconquista" of electric sound in the mid-1960s: Holmes 2007) had gained considerable experience either as session men, or as singers in the Chad Mitchell Trio, the New Christy Minstrels, or Lex Baxter's Balladeers (Rogan 1991); John Sebastian (who had big folk-rock hits with the Lovin' Spoonful) was a sought-after session musician in New York; Neil Young and Stephen Stills (Buffalo Springfield) had played the coffeehouse circuit, as had Jerry Garcia (Grateful Dead); and the Mamas and the Papas had been minor figures in their local folk scenes (Unterberger 2000). In most cases, these musicians, who were adequately trained, already accustomed to a market-oriented logic of cultural production, and with few symbolic resources in the smaller scene, saw the electrification of their music as a move that could bring more immediate and long-term rewards, at both the symbolic and the material levels.

Dylan's situation was different, because he had already acquired a central position in the revival, and, therefore, there were strong constraints on his making autonomous decisions about the style in which he could perform and the timing of a transition to electric music. At the time of the *Freewheelin' Bob Dylan* sessions, he had recorded a few electric tracks with a group of musicians, but the music sounded like an electrified jug band, so Dylan, John Hammond, and Albert Grossman felt it wasn't the right time or way to "go electric." They decided to stick with acoustic folk. Given these antecedents, it is quite surprising that Dylan's first forays into rock went mostly unnoticed. To the folk scene, as Silber noted and others repeated, the "new" Dylan was the one who had renounced protest and not the one who was going to plug in. Therefore, the controversy over Dylan's turn stressed the political rather than the aesthetic aspects of the folk revival's self-constructed "politics of style." As a student contributor wrote in *Broadside*, "his new songs, as performed at Newport, surprised everyone, leaving the majority of the audience annoyed, some even disgusted, and, in general, scratching its collective head in disbelief" (Wolfe 1964, 11). Although this is a review of Newport 1964, every single word could as effectively describe Newport 1965. Paul Wolfe, the author of these notes on the new Dylan, in comparing Phil Ochs's political songwriting with Dylan's new songs, points to a set of oppositions that —by the second half of 1964—marked the distance between Dylan on one side and the new breed of topical songwriters and his former supporters on the other: "meaning vs innocuousness, sincerity vs utter disregard for the tastes of the audience, idealistic principle vs self-conscious egotism" (Wolfe 1964, 11).

To Wolfe and other critics, Dylan turned to electric music because he had been contaminated by an "inauthentic" desire for fame, and the negative signs of his "selling out" had anticipated an electric turn. The lack of authenticity was identifiable in songs like "Chimes of Freedom" and "My Back Pages" (today lauded as some of Dylan's early classics), but also in the new direction that "Mr. Tambourine Man" was tracing. The debate about Dylan bloomed across several issues of *Broadside,* and for every Paul Wolfe, who thought that "Mr. Tambourine Man," "while underlain by a beautiful poetic idea, must be termed a failure," a "forced monotony of rhymes" (Wolfe 1964, 11), there was a Phil Ochs willing to support Dylan and point out to his critics that "it is as if the entire folk community was a huge biology class and Bob was a rare, prize frog" (Ochs 1965, 9). Ochs, indeed, countered that Dylan's new compositions, like "It Ain't Me, Babe" were "masterpieces of personal statement that have as great a significance as any of his protest material," concluding with a question that probably bewildered some revivalists: "How can anyone be so pretentious as to set guidelines for an artist to follow" (Ochs 1965, 9)? Yet this paternalistic approach had been dominant in the folk scene and was a legacy of its Popular Front days. Branding Dylan as inauthentic was almost an automatic reflex, coming from this political orientation, according to which artists were judged by "their social significance rather than by their art," as Serge Denisoff wrote quite frankly in an article for *Broadside* significantly titled "Dylan: Hero or Villain?" (Denisoff 1965).

Such was the debate in the spring and summer of 1965 that urged many in the folk revival to take sides, when Dylan had already released *Bringing It All Back Home,* "Subterranean Homesick Blues," and "Like a Rolling Stone." What Newport changed in the picture is that, all of a sudden, performance—and not simply electricity or politics—became an important criterion for the public evaluation of Dylan's authenticity. The opposition between electric and acoustic became a point of contention over tensions that had previously focused on poetics and politics. The new focus, however, meant a total reconfiguration of the debate, because Dylan's new approach to performance posed a more explicit threat to the authenticity of the revival, dissolving one coalition of entrepreneurs and creating a new one (Fine 2001).

The protagonists of the controversy had plenty of material to analyze and criticize. In June, The Byrds peaked at number one on the US charts, with their jingle-jangle rendition of "Mr. Tambourine Man," and other "pop" acts soon followed suit with "folk-rock" adaptations of Dylan's material (from Sonny and Cher to Frankie Valli and the Four Seasons), which were soon labeled "inauthentic," polarizing the factions of supporters and detractors of the new musical fad. As the Byrds were climbing up the charts, Dylan was busy for two days in the studio, cutting his aesthetic manifesto, "Like a Rolling Stone." Then, there was Newport, and in the aftermath of that concert, reactions flooded *Broadside*'s and *Sing Out!*'s mailboxes. Caryl Mirken, who attended the festival and wrote a review for *Broadside,* reported that Dylan, with "his black leather jacket, red shirt, tapered black slacks and electric guitar startled some in the audience and dismayed many," who soon found themselves in a "regular battle between boos and cheers" (Mirken 1965, 13). According to Joan Baez, "Bob was in a mess," although she also added that "he's really very good. People just don't understand his writing." Robert Shelton, always one of the most acute Dylan-watchers, sent his piece to the *New York Times* before Dylan took the stage, but he later returned to the subject, remarking that Dylan "introduced very unpersuasively his new fusion of folk and rock 'n' roll" (Shelton 1965a, xii). The debate triggered by Newport expanded into a new concept of folk music and into the difficult attempt to define a new subgenre, "folk-rock," which Shelton later identified as a trend that tried to marry rock and roll with "the folk movement's general concern for saying something about reality and injustice" (Shelton 1965b, 40).

To others, this fusion of genres was a sell-out to commercial logic. Once again, it was Silber who made some of the most explicit attacks on Dylan's new direction, and it was *Sing Out!,* the magazine in which the debate was hosted, that revealed the contrapositions that were tearing the folk scene apart. Newport and the release of *Bringing It All Back Home* and *Highway 61 Revisited* were perceived as two facets of Dylan's disaffiliation with his audience, his coalition of supporters, and ultimately the "Movement."[5]

Silber's criticism of Dylan went even further than the *cahier de doléances* that had characterized the open letter of 1964. He complained about the "opportunistic chaos" of the festival's finale, and even though he did not blame Dylan for that, he certainly had a few reservations that he made clear when he described the "most controversial scene" of the weekend. Dylan's electric set, he claimed, had divided him from the audience, because to many, "it seemed that it was not very good rock, while other disappointed legions did not think it was very good Dylan, while a few booed their once-and-former idol" (reprinted in McGregor 1990, 71). Dylan, who had emerged from "his cult-imposed aura of mystery" to showcase the top forty commercial music, had backed down, and Silber was one of the many on the scene to recognize that the acoustic performance of "It's All Over Now Baby Blue" was at once a swan song and a bitter farewell.

Paul Nelson, on the contrary, focused on the breach and the crisis that Dylan's performance had caused at Newport, extending its significance beyond the local setting and hinting at deeper reasons. Dylan provided, Nelson wrote, "the most dramatic scene I've ever witnessed in folk music" (reprinted in McGregor 1990, 73). Dylan's performance had forced people to choose sides, and Nelson was explicit in his identification of the figures around whom the formerly united folk revival was polarizing.

> Newport 1965, interestingly enough, split apart forever the two biggest names in folk music: Pete Seeger, who saw in Sunday night a chance to project this vision of the world and sought to have all others convey his impression (thereby restricting

their performances), and Bob Dylan, like some fierce Spanish outlaw in dress leather jacket. (75)

Nelson reluctantly admitted that people had chosen Seeger and "booed Dylan off the stage for something as superficially silly as an electric guitar or as stagnatingly sickening as their idea of owning an artist" (reprinted in McGregor 1990, 75). To Nelson, the politics and the aesthetics of the presentation by the performer went hand in hand; the remarks on the leather jacket and the electric guitar, as extensions of the personality and values of the performer, are notable, as is the overall tone of regret about the rejection of Dylan by the audience. It was, he claimed, a rejection of innovation, against which he was going to stand by choosing Dylan, his "art" and his "new songs." Given the delay in the publication of the always financially struggling *Sing Out!*, the controversy lasted months, even after Dylan had finally left the field and released his new, fully electric, *Highway 61 Revisited*. Nelson and Silber—in their reviews of the record for *Sing Out!*—were the main advocates of opposite visions, yet they still carried their battle against each other's position from within the field of the revival, and with reference to its cultural assumptions, codes, and deep narratives. Ironically, Silber was much more inclined to acknowledge that Dylan was doing something radically different and new, and Nelson's counterarguments still contained a plea for the acceptance of a transition that he thought was still totally internal to the folk scene: *Highway 61 Revisited* was, after all, "one of the two or three greatest folk music albums ever made" (McGregor 1990, 104–107).

The drama that Dylan's electric set inaugurated could not, like often happens in cases of social confrontation, be sealed off quickly. The breach was extended beyond the local occurrence, and it was recognized as an "event" that marked a turning point in the internal history of the folk revival. Everybody had to take a stand and offer an interpretation of both Dylan (and his image) and the event that had sparked the controversy. In the process, meanings and deep values came to the center, and contention focused mostly on Dylan's image rather than on his merits and faults. This debate was not limited to the close circle of writers and readers of folk fanzines. By the time *Highway 61 Revisited* was released, Dylan was to embark on an American and world tour, where, night after night, he had to confront on stage his departure from his former audience and his creation of a new one.

Forest Hills and the Presentation of a Multivocal Dylan

Dylan himself seemed very vocal in this debate, even though his interviews were often oblique. In the *Panorama* interview with Joseph Haas, he was quick to dismiss the label folk-rock, preferring quite ironically to describe his music as "just instruments" (reprinted in McGregor 1990, 108); Nat Hentoff's interview for *Playboy* (published in 1966) contained similar remarks, as Dylan was aware that "I don't think that such a word as folk-rock has anything to do with it. And folk music is a word I can't use" (McGregor 1990, 129–130), though he did not reach the height of songwriter Tom Paxton's sarcasm, who mocked it as "folk-rot" in the pages of *Sing Out!* (Paxton 1966). Dylan, indeed, still perceived authenticity as a very important resource in this war of position: in his interview with Nora Ephron and Susan Edmiston, which is one of the most valuable documents concerning Dylan in the middle of this transitional phase, he still praised the authenticity of folk songs. "Folk music is the only music where it isn't simple. It's never been simple. It's weird, man, full of legends, myths, Bible, and ghosts" (Cott 2006, 50). At the same time, however, he drew a line between authentic traditional folk and seemingly inauthentic protest or topical music. In other words, Dylan was still using the vocabulary of authenticity and trying to project an image of authenticity that could bypass the folk–rock debate and define an autonomous niche where his music could be categorized.

The world tour was—as the title of one bootleg suggests—a "nightly ritual," full of sacred fervor and contaminations, of threats to authenticity and questions about identities. Not surprisingly, it started like Newport had ended, with a mix of boos and praise, of acoustic music and electricity. Dylan had probably planned to go fully electric, but following the advice of his manager, Albert Grossman, he finally decided for a half acoustic, half electric, long concert of about ninety minutes. The concerts themselves were staged in such a way as to puzzle the audience and defy easy categorization. The concerts, thus, were carefully scripted in their structure to signify in public the transition Dylan had already made at Newport, but with a reversal in the order of his performance, beginning with acoustic and ending with electric. A look at Dylan's setlist for the debut show at Forest Hills is useful to gain insight into the careful balance that existed between different visions of the artist as the subject of performance and into the way he was willing to articulate his new, transitional self.

> Acoustic Set: She Belongs To Me; To Ramona; Gates Of Eden; Love Minus Zero / No Limit; Desolation Row; It's All Over Now, Baby Blue; Mr. Tambourine Man
> Intermission
> Electric Set: Tombstone Blues; I Don't Believe You (She Acts Like We Never Have Met); From A Buick 6; Just Like Tom Thumb's Blues; Maggie's Farm; It Ain't Me, Babe; Ballad Of A Thin Man; Like A Rolling Stone

The songs were from his three most recent albums, and Dylan did not play any songs associated with his protest phase. As a musical retrospective of his work, it covered only the albums that had been either criticized for their introvert, existentialist lyrics, or rejected outright for their use of electric instruments. By all means, this was the setlist a sell-out would play. Except for "Like a Rolling Stone," all the tracks from *Highway 61 Revisited* (numbers 5, 8, 10, 11, and 14) got their live debut two days before the official release of the album, and only three of the songs (numbers 2, 9, and 13) came from his acoustic phase.

If one needs any evidence that Dylan was in a trench fighting for his own recognition, the concert at Forest Hills provides plenty, being one of the most heated moments when the "new" Dylan was simultaneously rejected by his audience and symbolically degraded as a polluted figure who could not attempt to give shape to his new claims about authenticity. The trouble began even before Dylan appeared on stage for the first half of the show. Murray the K, a famous deejay associated with pop music, who was emceeing for the concert, was booed as soon as he was introduced on the stage. His hip talk was interrupted several times by boos and catcalls from the audience, especially when he claimed that what they were going to see was something totally new: "It's not rock, it's not folk, it's a new thing called Dylan."

Forest Hills was a performance wrapped in these dilemmas of presentation of the artist's new persona and communication to the audience. After Newport, the commonsense view of Dylan's alleged betrayal was that the issues at stake were more the medium and the style (electric vs. acoustic) than the content. Therefore, when Dylan appeared on stage with just his acoustic guitar and harmonicas, he was met with a supportive roar from the entire audience. The normal indications of affiliation (including the audience's silence during the songs) worked for the first half of the show, because the image Dylan projected was consistent with the one that had been shaped in the context of the folk scene: the use of a traditional means of expression (the acoustic guitar), the poetic tone of his lyrics, and the clear enunciation (Dylan's image as an important young poet overshadowed his reputation as a singer) all worked to create his legitimacy as a performer and generated the impression of his authenticity within the performance.

But one has only to listen to what happened in the intermission to realize that the alignment between artist and audience that was automatically created during the acoustic set was suddenly shattered. As soon as the band walked on stage and Al Kooper started to play the electric piano, the first booing was heard. The band then tried to find a groove for "Tombstone Blues," and Dylan could sing only a couple of lines before the audience revolted. It was the first of many instances of audience disaffiliation during the electric set. Then silence—maybe an astonished silence—dominated the arena, until Dylan and the band reached the end of the song, at its first public presentation.

What very little applause there was, was buried by loud boos, which soon gave way to louder catcalls, when Dylan offered the first electric arrangement of an acoustic song, "I Don't Believe You." As soon as the band reached the end of the song, the battle for identity began. The separation between Dylan and the audience took the shape of a call for the real Dylan, which had been hidden or silenced by the decision to be backed by a band. "We want Dylan" was a common call both at Newport and Forest Hills, though its meaning was decidedly different. At Forest Hills, Dylan was on stage, and the yells were aimed at denying Dylan any right to shape his new self and presentation. The real Dylan, the one they knew, or so the audience claimed, had to be brought back; in order to achieve this goal, the new Dylan had to become the object of a ritual of degradation that redefined his identity (Garfinkel 1956). The catcalls were thus an act of denunciation, and Dylan was in the uncomfortable position of the denounced person, a total reversal of the way the ceremonial, ritual, and performative aspects of a concert are usually constructed. The denunciation also took the shape of a triadic structured confrontation. As Garfinkel reminds us, the process of degradation involves the simultaneous presence of a denouncer (the angry audience), a denounced (the electric Dylan, in this case), and a public that must assess the nature and the implications of the violation. The audience that supported Dylan was this local public, but it was mostly a public of witnesses and not a public involved in the defense of the artist. Dylan had dismissed early on his audience's attempt to attack him. He had instructed the members of his band to continue playing no matter what happened on stage, because he was sure that there was going to be some confrontation with the audience. Dylan denied his opponents in the audience the social power to take over the performance. He countered the calls for the "real Dylan" to appear with a sarcastic, "Aw, come on!" and that was the only communication he had with the audience.

In his review for the *New York Times,* Shelton added that the disaffiliation between the artist and the public was not just audible, it was also visible. The people who contested Dylan tried to break the boundaries of presentation that usually kept the artist and the audience separated. In other words, they tried to get in control of liminal zones, but also of the territory of performance, the stage itself (Al Kooper was knocked off his seat by an enraged fan during "Just Like Tom Thumb's Blues" or "It Ain't Me, Babe"), and several members of the audience, as Shelton wrote, "ran onto a roped-off grass section in front of the stage, after, or during, songs. Several eluded the guards and got to the stage." Dylan, on his part, "kept his coolness" (Shelton 1965c, 20).

Toward the end of the concert (which had no encores), the polarization became wider and reached a climax when Dylan performed a new "folk-rock" version of "It Ain't Me,

Babe," another song that speaks indifferently about a lover and the audience. The audience's disapproval met—for one rare moment—with some applause, but the newly found connection disappeared when Dylan started singing the refrain. First, more catcalls, then (on the second refrain) the audience started to sing along: was it a sign of affiliation or an instance of appropriation of the artist's work to mark a distance, indicating that he was not what they were looking for? Probably the latter, because the booing and the heckling started again when the song ended and reached momentum during an interminably long introduction to "Ballad of a Thin Man." Then, the only miracle of the night—"Like a Rolling Stone." The roles reversed, and huge applause praised the final song of the concert, Dylan's own cathartic experience, his biggest hit up to that moment, and a much stronger version than the one played at Newport. The audience sang along, "How does it feel?," and by the second verse the words were floating in the air, thanks to a thousand voices, a fact that prompted Shelton to close his review pointing out that "Evidently the hostility extends only towards things with which they aren't familiar," and praised Dylan's ability to conquer in the end "an unruly audience" (Shelton 1965c, 20).

However, in the Forest Hills performance, we can witness more than the attempt on Dylan's part to proselytize his audience. The audience and the artist were two parties in a confrontation that could not reach a synthesis. Both the artist and the audience were articulating within the local setting of the performance their own take on identity and were reconfiguring the meanings that had suddenly been exposed at Newport. Taken from this point of view, the performance was an occasion to work simultaneously on preferred readings of the image of the artist, on the deeper semiotic structure on which it rested, and on the feelings and experiences associated with performance. As Dylan moved on—first at the Hollywood Bowl and then across the country—the structure that had made the folk revival stable was coming to the surface of the performance. It wasn't an alternative between acoustic and electric anymore; rather, it was a total involvement in the redefinition of a new politics of style, genre, message, and subject. Yet more was to follow, in the form of success and in the form of further, almost violent battles over the definition of the artist as a symbol and the definition of the self.

The Ghost of Authenticity

Questions about identity challenged Dylan. The electric turn was a debate about identity as much as it was a debate about music, where what happened on stage and what was circulated through different media became a dialogue that shaped practices of support and disaffiliation during the concerts and provided proof of Dylan's uncomfortable status for many sectors of his audience. Dylan carried all the ambivalences that characterize liminal figures—those figures that are involved in a transition and cannot be categorized according to a recognizable status (Turner 1969), and who are suspended in a sort of "betwixt and between" condition. Even the most liminal figures, however, are created against a background of available representations, which come from previous experience and from symbols and practices that are rooted in a group's culture. Dylan's trajectories as a poet and as a perceived prophet—within and outside the folk revival—stand out as typical examples of this dynamic, which can create representations that stick with the public and limit the way an artist is perceived.

The consolidation of public images not only creates visible characteristics that serve to categorize the artist and possibly identify him as the bearer of a "style" or as the preeminent representative of a certain genre. It can also backfire and prevent further efforts on the artist's part to produce radically new work, to extend his fan base, or to adjust his image according to a new context.[6] Labels are important as shortcuts for these complex processes of categorization, and in 1965 and early 1966 the labels attached to Dylan worked in two opposite directions: on the one hand, the artist could engage in the production of a charismatic narrative in order to challenge and reject already available categories; on the other, previous representations affected the recognition of Dylan and oriented public judgments about the artist and his performances.

When these tensions occur, image-trouble can bring unforeseen dangers. Figures who acquire a symbolic status—as

sociologist Orrin Klapp reminded us back in the 1960s—
"function through [their] meaning or image," and their symbolic characteristics are made and unmade by what Klapp
identifies as "dramatic encounters" (Klapp 1964, 7) with
the audience. As I showed in the previous chapter, Dylan's
authenticity was constructed within a circle that held together production and reception, and—similarly—Dylan's
claims about a new authenticity had to pass through the
same ordeal of symbolic evaluation. Previous images can
be burdensome in moments of transition and can be appropriated by interested parties to counter an artist's claims
about authenticity, drawing a line between an authentic self
that has been dismissed and a new, inauthentic image. The
image of the old Dylan was indeed exploited in the war of
position about electricity both on stage and in the critical
reviews that seemed to pile up and attack Dylan soon after
the release of "Like a Rolling Stone."

A particularly scathing review was published in the *Melody
Maker*, one of Britain's bibles for all things music. According to Bob Dawbarn, who published his long review in the
August 7, 1965, issue of the *Melody Maker*, "Like a Rolling
Stone" could not "hold the interest for what seems like the
six longest minutes since the invention of time" (Dawbarn
1965). The problem came—according to the reviewer—from
Dylan's attempt to fill too many roles simultaneously, thus
disappointing several sectors of his audience while not gaining any new ground in terms of aesthetic accomplishment
and commercial appeal: "His talents have become so diffuse
—folksinger, writer with a social conscience, composer of
hit songs, poet, satirist, pop star. The trouble comes when
he starts mixing the roles," delivering "sub-standard Dylan.
And that is what 'Like a Rolling Stone' is!" (Dawbarn 1965).
One month later, "Like a Rolling Stone" hit number 2 on the
charts, and Dylan started his tour at Forest Hills. But the
controversy, rather than settling down, became bigger as
the concerts finally provided an opportunity to voice competing claims about Dylan's identity, which seized on the
multiplicity of social images that Dawbarn had stigmatized
in his review.

During the performance, the audience reactions were
asymmetrically distributed, giving the impression that the
two sets Dylan played (acoustic and with the band) were two

different environments that were governed by a totally different pattern of reception and recognition. Dylan's acoustic concerts in 1965 resembled consistently the kind of polite celebration of the artist on stage that Ray Coleman depicted in his review of a show in Leicester: "When this slight, serious faced and incredibly casual man walked onstage—with a guitar, seven harmonicas and two glasses of water his only company—there was silence. At the end of every song, the audience applauded—thunderously. No screams, no whistles, no talking. The applause almost switched off almost mechanically, like it was canned" (Coleman 1965). Dylan's status as a sort of high priest was shaped locally in the performance by this sort of behavior that produced a distance between the artist and the audience. In the acoustic sets, Dylan positioned himself closer to his former folk persona, not contaminated by the pop craziness that characterized the Beatles and the Rolling Stones, the acts to which the "rock" Dylan was always unfavorably compared, like in the review that Charles Champlin wrote in September 1965 for the *Los Angeles Times*: "The monumental difference [from the shows the Beatles had just played at the Hollywood Bowl] was that this vast audience paid singer Bob Dylan the compliment of pin-drop silence while he was performing. His rewards thereafter were thunderous applause, a scattering of whistles but no screams, which is interesting because there was obviously at least a partial overlap between his audience and the Beatles'" (Champlin 1965, D12).

But when Dylan came back for the electric half, Champlin remarked, it was almost evident that Newport "had the right idea," because the effect of the "added sound" was to "undercut Dylan's individuality, putting him into a bag" with other pop performers (Champlin 1965, D12). The alternative between an acoustic Dylan and an electric Dylan was thus perceived as a relevant opposition between the place the artist deserved as a consequence of his talent, and the place he was trying to occupy as a sign of his surrender to a commercial logic. The fact that Dylan performed as what his critics perceived to be his "natural" self, the artist, the poet, and the folk minstrel, night after night, kept this image alive and ready for exploitation by opponents. However, this image was also questioned during the shows, not least by the artist himself, as he made the transition visible every time the folksinger returned to the stage with his band. The performance of the "new Dylan" for the electric set kept almost nothing of the acoustic singer who had stunned the audience just a few minutes before. The electric show was staged, scripted, and performed to signal a total departure from the acoustic set. Whereas Dylan performed the latter according to the rules he had followed for years, and which were shaped in such a way as to put him at the center of the performance, the entrance of the electric Dylan meant a total reconfiguration of the artist's performative role: Dylan was screaming, jumping, holding the microphone with his hands and waving his hands to stress the importance of what he was singing on the stage. It was, in other words, a performance that was aimed at showing, on a nightly basis, the death and the rebirth of the artist, and to substitute one image with another.[7]

The theme of ritual death was, indeed, explored and voiced by those sectors of the audience that explicitly accused Dylan of selling out. By marking the distinction between an authentic and an inauthentic Dylan, the sectors of the audience that felt and expressed a disaffiliation with Dylan were able to produce a narrative of decay that stressed—as a crucial point—the reversal of Dylan's role and his fall into the domain of symbolic contamination. Some letters to *Sing Out!* and to other papers, often written in the aftermath of Dylan's shows, provide good evidence of this black-or-white attitude toward Dylan.[8] The criticism against Dylan reprised the themes already articulated by Silber and others: the loss of authenticity, the shift from collectivism to individualism, the aesthetic threat on folk purity. One Kathleen Ivans from New York stigmatized Dylan's transition by introducing a vocabulary of social death: "Folk fans the world over are mourning the death of Bob Dylan, who died at Carnegie Hall on Oct. 1, 1965. In a short but brilliant career, Mr. Dylan amassed fans and fame with his electrifying performances. He leaves a legacy of only four albums which contain some of the best folk music ever written." Others claimed that Dylan's Newport set had "nothing to do with art or humanism—and even less to do with folk music," or accused Dylan of being a "commercial enterprise." On the contrary, Dylan's *Sing Out!* supporters justified their position (and what they thought was Dylan's) with reference to the same vocabulary of authenticity and the progressive character of folk. The "oral tradition," one claimed, was "in the hands of top 40 radio." The clash was within folk, between moving forward and the old vision of the scene: if people wanted pure, unstained folk—Polly Demuth wrote in her letter—"they can go into the hills and listen to some ignorant cowboy singing about dad's old whiskey still."

Dylan's contested reputation was shaped by both fields in such a way that the contenders could use the repertoire of authenticity that was typical of the folk scene, and especially of the urban folk of the 1960s (Demuth's comment is impressive because she dismissed in a line all the rhetoric of the Other that people like Alan Lomax had tightly connected to the folk revival from the 1930s to the 1960s). To some extent, Dylan's folk reputation framed the reception of the electric turn within and outside of the concerts and created expectations, especially in audiences in Australia, France, and Great Britain, where the artist had been branded (and marketed) by promoters with reference to the narrative that had been produced in the folk revival, with little mention of the transition that Dylan had already made visible and public in the United States.

The tour booklet for the Australian tour featured a portrait of Dylan under the title "The Tambourine Man," and a reproduction of Dylan's Guthrie-esque poem "My Life in a Stolen Moment."[9] Dylan was still praised as "the best folk musician," although the controversy that he had created since 1965 was not a part of the corporate production of Dylan's image: "Rumor is that the purists are grumbling and sulking about the electric guitars and about the 'obscurity' of the lyrics, but can they really be listening?" The short blurb featured on the British concert program went even further in stressing Dylan's folk identity:

> Bob Dylan has systematically shaken, upset, overturned, and finally re-routed the entire course of contemporary folk music. There isn't a singer in the folk field today who wasn't in some way influenced by him, in his writing, his performing, even in his appearance. The imitators are legion, but Dylan continues on his own way, belonging to no-one, blazing his own trails—exciting, unpredictable, unexcelled.

Similarly, the tour booklet for the concert in Paris featured the *New Yorker* interview with Nat Hentoff that described the *Another Side of Bob Dylan*'s recording session. Dylan's folk reputation stood as a powerful constraint on his attempt to perform the transition, and the stark contrast between the folk Dylan and the rock Dylan became a core theme of the narrative constructed around the concerts, as well as something that had to be performed both by the artist and by the audience.

To some extent, thus, Dylan's image during the world tour —even more than in the United States—still bore powerful traces of the persona he had rejected and which had been evaluated and dissected in the first months of the electric turn. The media, with which Dylan played incessantly in a number of press conferences that soon turned into performances in their own right, were pushing this image, creating thus a competing claim about the artist and his authenticity. Accounts of the concerts, in other words, became a mediated instance where Dylan's reputation was exposed and simultaneously shaped. Sociologist David Pattie argues, on this point, that performance and mediatization are always in a dialogue and are not part of a binary dialectic: "liveness and replication exist in dialogue—and that dialogue is not simply between the authentic and the mediatised. Rather, the dialogue is between the performers, the technology that surrounds them ..., the audience, the industry, the wider culture, the history of the band, of the event, and of the form" (Pattie 2007, 23). What Pattie should add, however, is that this dialogue is always enacted in concrete instances, and only retrospectively can we identify a unifying narrative that compresses meanings into a recognizable form. In the midst of the events, this dialogue is a free-flow exchange that reduces the uncertainty of the social process of performance and contributes to the creation of a set of mutual expectations on the part of the audience, and on the part of the artist. As Dylan's case shows, this dialogue does not necessarily have to be consensual; it might be sufficient to draw a common ground for contention, for the definition of the concert itself as the setting of disaffiliation, and for a series of repertoires to be "broadcast" to the public as guidelines for the expression of conflict against or affiliation with the artist.

Many, almost all, news reports about Dylan's electric tour narrate a very simple and puzzling story: a person who had once been an idol is under attack from his audience, and the shows into which he has put great effort to reveal his new identity (an identity that the artist proclaimed to be an authentic one) are panned as a "critical" disaster, where the hero turns into a villain and is subject to symbolic degradation while on the stage. Why and how, then, was Dylan able to survive this ordeal that could have destroyed anyone else's image and career? In the next section, I will argue that symbolic conflict, the alignment with emerging values, and Dylan's ability to fight the battle with his audience, provided elements for the production and distribution of the charismatic narrative that has since been attached to the "electric turn." Analyzing the patterns of mobilization of the audience in this context seems to be very important to understanding this dynamic of incorporation of controversy as a positive element of Dylan's image and artistic reputation.

"Play Fucking Loud!": Mobilization, Confrontation, and Disaffiliation on the Road to the Free Trade Hall

Abroad, audiences were barely aware of the changes in the coalition that supported Dylan in his homeland, or of the effects of the emergence of folk-rock in redefining authenticity, the popular, and notions of identity and belonging to the scene. As he left for Australia, where he played a few concerts prior to a European tour, the tension between the old and the new, and between the proposal of the artist and the reception of the public, lost any reference to the transformation that was affecting both Dylan and the folk revival. Folk-rock (whatever it meant at the time) could hardly be a point of reference, neither in Australia nor in Europe, and the dominant perception of Dylan as a folk artist affected his reception both in the venues and in the reviews. In Australia, Dylan was usually more talkative than in the United States, and he tried to captivate the audience on several occasions, including a moment in Melbourne when he was able to make his audience laugh as he proclaimed boldly that he was indeed playing "a folk music guitar."

The reception of the electric sets, as usual, was much more mixed. Of Melbourne, one who was there remembered:

> I remember more catcalls (than boos), people yelling insults. There were a lot of people who quite deliberately and conspicuously walked out as soon as the musicians walked onstage after intermission. Like they'd sat through the intermission so they could make this walk out protest thing. I am pretty sure I can remember people holding up signs too. (Lee 2004b, 78)

These three forms of mobilization within the concerts (yelling insults, walking out, and holding up signs) offered a counter-performance to Dylan's and contested the scripts that the artist tried to articulate during the performance. They also affected the local asymmetry of power that is necessary to "create" the artist as the center of the performance. The performative asymmetry—and the creation of a symbolic focus—are necessary conditions for the production of an effective performance or ritual. The artist usually serves as a symbol of the wider social group and becomes the center of emotions and action. However, emotional and performative disaffiliation create a strain in the performance, and their public expression threatens the order of the performance. The asymmetry of interaction, which deals with the legitimacy of the artist to claim that he is the center of attention in the performance, is often put into question by local incidents (think about the invasion of the stage and the way it is usually highly regulated through the interaction of audience, artist, and gatekeepers like the security). However, the artist usually has the power to restore the local order that has been disrupted. What happened in Australia (and, as we shall see, in Europe) did not follow this trend, especially because Dylan had no way to control the actions of the audience.

Nowhere did the mobilization of the audience reach such a high point of contestation of Dylan's claims to authenticity as it did in Great Britain (Lee 2009). Dylan had had a very warm reception when he toured Britain in 1965, and he had stunned the British audience. The endorsement from the Beatles and popular covers by the Animals and Manfred Mann had exposed the audience to a beat version of folk-rock. The Byrds, moreover, had topped the charts with "Mr. Tambourine Man," although their reception in England had been lukewarm. When he arrived in England for the European leg of the world tour, however, Dylan was ready to be confronted by his audience with the same animosity that had characterized the Australian tour. The folk revival was much stronger and pressed for more ideological "purity" than anywhere else, especially as a consequence of the folk revival's close connection to the cultural policy of the British Communist Party (Brocken 2003, 43–66). To some in the field of Dylan's supporters, the British tour was a "crusade," and the concerts were—to say the least—a "critical disaster" (Shelton 1986, 366).[10]

Critics and enraged sectors of the audience, indeed, jumped on Dylan, and rumors about the bad reception of the concerts soon reached other concertgoers, who by the time Dylan closed the World Tour knew—to some extent— what was expected of them: to voice their dissatisfaction and degrade the artist publicly. The polarized reception of the two sets—respect and hostility—became the common script that the audience followed, and Dylan had to make his way through the powerful and exhilarating electric sets in the midst of the audiences' explicit attempts to delegitimize his music, his band, and his character. In Dublin, shouts of "traitor" broke out, as *Disc and Music Echo* reported (no recording of the electric set is available) (cited in Shelton 1986, 366). The *Melody Maker* (the voice of the music establishment) found it "unbelievable to see a hip-swinging Dylan trying to look and sound like Mick Jagger." A letter to the *Melody Maker Magazine* announced that the writer had witnessed "a funeral at Bristol's Colston Hall. They buried Bob Dylan, the Folk-singer, in a grave of electric guitars, enormous speakers, and deafening drums. It was a sad end to one of the most phenomenal influences in music. My only consolation, Woody Guthrie wasn't there to witness it" (cited in Lee 2004b, 84–85). Jagger and Guthrie were two opposite views of "artist" that Dylan was desperately trying to meld in an attempt to define himself as an artist. The folk sector thought that by abandoning Guthrie and trying to reach the electric superstardom of Jagger, Dylan was admitting on stage that he had sold out and that he had betrayed the ideals and values of the folk revival. Accordingly, their charges against Dylan were more on moral grounds than on aesthetic and performative ones. In Birmingham Dylan met with walkouts and cries of "traitor," "Give us the real Dylan," "we want folk," and the headline on the *Mail and Dispatch* read, "Dylan, the legend, disappoints."

That Dylan was not exactly playing "folk," to a relevant part of the audience, did not matter. What mattered during the acoustic sets and was instrumental in making them a safe territory for performance, was the selection of an appropriate script, which was consistent with his image for the traditionalist or purist public (the acoustic guitar and the harmonica). Yet one should also note that the stage was simultaneously set for something different, and the electric instruments (the drum set, the organ, and the piano) were visible on stage, hinting at what was to come. To some extent, the acoustic set, which many regarded as the highlight of the night, the reason they were there, and the only evidence Dylan could provide that he still had some glimpse of "authenticity," was only a transitional moment that led to the electric set.

If we compare what usually happened during the intermission with the polite reverence with which the audience listened to the acoustic set, it almost seems like they were two different concerts. In terms of the management of the performance by the artist, they certainly were. The boundary between the artist and the audience became wider, and there was a performative reversal that led many to address their discontent directly toward Dylan and deny him any autonomy to choose the kind of performance he was willing to offer. In Bristol, right after the performance of "I Don't Believe You," a member of the audience shouted quite politely: "Would you turn the volume down, *please*?" to which Dylan responded, with an immediacy that was not present in the acoustic set: "You don't like rock 'n' roll?" And in Birmingham, to the people asking "for some folk music," he replied sarcastically (as quoted by Lee 2004b), "If you want some folk music, I'll play you some folk music. This is a folksong my grandaddy used to play for me. . . . It goes like this" (Lee 2004b, 86).

And the rock version of "Baby, Let Me Follow You Down," followed. It was indeed a folk song. But Dylan's arrangement enraged many in the audience, because of what they perceived as his traitorous attempts to touch and pollute the ideas of preservation and authenticity that the song stood for with his electric guitars. The students' magazine of the University of Birmingham *Red Brick* (May 18, 1966) offered a different report, though the exchange is more or less the same:

> The man in the second half was not the Bob Dylan the audience had come for. He was the shell of a man who has gained the whole world but had lost his soul. From behind an electric guitar and backed by a five-piece band he endured heckling from the audience. "Now I'll sing you a folk song," said the shell "that ma Grand-daddy sang to ma mother when she was a little girl." If his mother had heard what followed the chances are that Bob would never have been born even. He introduced the next piece as "Yes I see you, you've got your brand new leopard-skin pill box hat." The connection between Dylan and "folk" was finally broken. The crowning atrocity was yet to come in the form of "One Too Many Mornings" which most of his followers remember as the real "Dylan." I was contemplating the Exit as the electric guitar and organ took it and strangled the soul from it. (Lee 2004b)

Indeed, the two songs that sparked the most bitter confrontation during the electric set were usually "Baby, Let Me Follow You Down" and "One Too Many Mornings," both closely associated to the old, acoustic Dylan. They are the first instances of what would become Dylan's constant rearrangement and transformation of his songs. But in the context of the electric turn, those changes seemed to many nothing less than open betrayal, the attempt to make profane that which was viewed as pure—sacred, traditional folk and the old Dylan.

In Liverpool, things went even worse. The crowd started the slow hand-clapping (supreme degradation of an artist in England), and insults lasted for two minutes between "Just Like Tom Thumb's Blues" and "Leopard-Skin Pill-Box Hat," to the point that Dylan had to announce the latter song twice. The concert had started in a similar way, with someone asking, "Where's Bob Dylan?" after "Tell Me, Momma," and reached a climax after "One Too Many Mornings," which was as controversial as usual. Somebody shouted, "Where's the poet in you?" Dylan replied coldly, "There's a fellow up there looking for the savior. The savior is backstage." Leicester, Sheffield, Edinburgh, even Paris (where the audience voiced its rage about the huge American flag appearing backstage) were stations of this type of confrontation. But the performance that is inscribed most deeply in memory is Manchester, May 17, 1966, a performance that became only slightly less famous than Newport, after the first bootleg recording appeared in the early seventies.

Manchester was a condensation of all the tensions that had split Dylan and a sector of his audience apart since Newport and Forest Hills. Newport has acquired mythic status for symbolic reasons: it was the first electric gig; the setting was salient, the folk revival's sacred place of celebration; Dylan was booed. Manchester was one of the many instances of symbolic warfare during the British tour. It had been one of the first recordings to circulate, and so much tension and contention built up during the electric set, climaxing in an enraged member of the audience shouting, "Judas!" to Dylan. It was the ultimate offense to Dylan, and he, equally enraged, shouted back, "I don't believe you! You are a liar." An invitation for the band to "play fucking loud" followed, which could have come from Dylan, Robbie Robertson, or some supportive member of the audience. And indeed "Like a Rolling Stone" was loud, tight, and—as Greil Marcus has remarked with his usual understanding for the emotional nuances of Dylan's performances—a moment when "Dylan shoulders the song as if he has never felt such a burden in his life" (Marcus 2006, 183).

The ultimate denunciation created by the "Judas!" insult resulted in a definitive asymmetry, creating a negative distance instead of the positive one that is usually experienced between an artist and his supportive public. It was, in some respects, an exercise of power that is not usually scripted in a concert, but which the electric turn—and the appearance of Dylan as a wannabe rock star—allowed as a consequence of Dylan's repositioning. When actors undergo a transformation, and there are no fixed rules for the transition, both symbolic elevation of the individual and acts intended to reverse the individual's position can occur. And heckling works as a symbolic and very expressive means of shifting the balance of power in a performance, from the singer to the audience (Duffett 2009). The "Judas" comment was at the same time an act of degradation and an act of expulsion from a community, which condensed the fractures that had occurred between Dylan and his audiences since Newport into a micro-incident. It was, in some respects, the final act in defining the artist's identity, over which Dylan had only partial control.

What is interesting about this chain of events is that, although it had the potential to permanently harm Dylan's reputation and prevent his further success (it involved powerful sectors of his audience and an alignment with the mainstream media, and it was repeated over time), the outcome was reversed in a narrative of conquest that boosted Dylan's image and created important elements of the Dylan myth that has remained with the artist ever since.

Conclusions

To quote Dylan, sometimes "there is no success like failure." And to many, the electric turn was a failure in nearly every respect. Words like *betrayal* and *selling out* became common currency among Dylan's original fans. Yet Dylan's reputation as an innovator and his symbolic capital were increased by his decision to go electric. As I have tried to argue, many accounts of this transition fail to understand the performative dynamics, the fact that it was in performance, rather than in the records, that the turn was accomplished.

Dylan's representations of what performing music *meant* clashed with his audience's expectations of who he had to be and diverged from the standards of performing music that were held by his former audience. How did it come about, then, that he was successful in establishing his own image as a musical revolutionary? Here, the social processes of artistic reputation that are *embedded in* and not *external to* performance must be taken into account.

Why, then, do we now think of Dylan as a pioneer and of this world tour as a mythic narrative of rock music? To some extent, this must have to do with what actually happened during this tour and with the narratives that have been constructed around it over the last forty years. Performances always have some representational consequences that build an individual's reputation—the way he is perceived within a social field or a plurality of social fields.

Dylan was able to incorporate the contested and divided reception of his electric turn, because it was consistent with the key meaning he articulated in his performances, that of an artist actively seeking his individuality and producing a visible impression of the fracture between his effort and the narrative articulated by folk revivalists. As is any creative, transitional moment, though, this alignment to emergent meanings and changing audiences was potentially risky. Yet, the availability of cultural repertoires and the creation of a coalition that was able to support and broadcast them provided an opportunity for Dylan. Without them, he would have otherwise been trapped between the possibility of a new means of expression and the resistance of an older frame having different political and aesthetic values.

Forcing folk into bed with rock, then, seems to be more than just a suggestive metaphor. As I have tried to show, it was the essence of Dylan's effort, which can be understood properly only insofar as we consider how he concretely achieved this goal during his performances. These concerts were at once spaces for innovation, for tracing legitimate boundaries or breaking the constraints of genre, and for confrontation (ideological as well as aesthetic). A close look at performance can help bring an understanding of the social forces, the symbolic production, and the actual interaction through which these overwhelming tasks were accomplished. The outcome of this process was notable, because not only was Dylan able to emerge as a leading figure in popular music, he also reconfigured the standards for the evaluation of the artist at a time when other actors in the folk revival—mostly young critics and young musicians—were interested in making a similar transition.

Dylan entered this process as a recognized folk artist, and, by the end of the electric turn, he was nothing less than a star, highly successful from the commercial point of view and praised by critics and fellow musicians. This image has been with him ever since, constraining further changes in his career that were affected by the powerful presence of his symbolic traits as a 1960s musical revolutionary who accomplished these many transitions before the age of twenty-five. However, this period of transition was also the time a peculiar "Dylan myth" was created and broadcasted to larger audiences. In this process, the original network of supporters and detractors, and the original struggles about the definition of the artist as a symbol, were pushed to the background and silenced by the charismatic narrative that was built around Dylan. In some sense, Dylan's status as a symbol became relatively autonomous from the circumstances that had contributed to create it. The valence of the electric turn was reversed—from disaster to founding moment—and the Dylan controversy acquired the positive meaning of an individualist's struggle to establish new ideas about music and culture, for which Dylan is still celebrated. However, such a turn in public perception did not come without a cost to the artist, for Dylan's positioning as a revolutionary and indeed charismatic artist allowed this representation to be available for audiences anytime Dylan was perceived as an artist who did not live up to the expectations posed by these representations and perceptions.

In the following chapters, I will discuss how Dylan has had to deal with these constraints, and I will describe how performance has been an important means for the artist to assist in the creation of his own reputation and—ultimately—his memorialized image.

Notes

1. This appropriation of previous images of Dylan the moment he takes a sudden turn seems to be a lasting characteristic of Dylan's trajectory as an artist. Public images, indeed, are shaped collectively and are composed by complex representational traits that can be recombined (with differences in valence, salience, and claims to ownership) by interested parties (Jansen 2007). Some of these images remain more or less stable for a considerable amount of time, and they constrain interpretation of a figure. In some other cases (and Dylan's is a prominent example) efforts by the subject of these reputations can be contrasted by the reference (by audiences and other interested parties) to previous images that create a memory of the artist and the standards for the evaluation of alignment and detachment from the symbolic elements that constitute his reputation.

2. These micro-interactions *practically construct* Dylan's status as an artist in transition. During a performance, signs of affiliation and disaffiliation (like applause, yells, or booing) are less a way to display the position of the parties in an interaction than practices that create it (Clayman 1993), thus playing a performative role. Dylan's transition from the role of folksinger hero to the role of

rock star seems not just a movement across two different structural sectors of the popular music field, but also a very practical, and embodied, process that resulted from the interaction between artist and audience.

3. Bikel, on this occasion, drew the boundary with reference to a normative dimension very close to Durkheim's original argument about the absolute separation between the sacred and the profane (Durkheim 1995). Boundary work is essential not only to draw distinctions in classification, but also to produce feelings of identity in those who produce the classifications. For a general review, see Lamont and Molnar (2002).

4. For a scholarly appraisal of the artistic exchanges between Dylan and the Beatles, see especially Inglis (1996).

5. *Highway 61 Revisited* has been deservedly praised as a landmark moment in rock's history and as a turning point of Dylan's career. For an overview of the sessions, see Heylin (1995), Irwin (2008), and Polizzotti (2006).

6. Moving forward and being recognizable are two fundamental components of the trajectories of artists, the combination of which leads to very different outcomes that deserve a comparative analysis. Both traits have much to do with the visibility of the artist and the process of the reception of the representations that he—and other reputational entrepreneurs—produce in the public space. Dylan's case shows many instances of the tension that is created between these two aspects of the symbolization of an artist. What seems to be most striking, however, is the tight connection that exists between movement and permanence, and which has resulted in the durable representation according to which Dylan can be recognized as an artist as long as he keeps moving.

7. Unfortunately, footage from these concerts seems to be safe in Dylan's vaults. However, from the snippets that Martin Scorsese included in his documentary *No Direction Home,* one can get a clear idea of how Dylan defied all performative standards about the presentation of the artist that were part of the ideology of the folk revival and took on a rock persona in performances where these gestures were a fundamental part of the artist's self-definition and markers of his detachment from the rather restricted express rules that defined the artist's role in the revival.

8. All the quotations below—unless otherwise noted—are from McGregor (1990, 117–120).

9. These tour booklets have never been reprinted (and all the information presented here is taken from copies that are part of my personal collection), but they are important documents for understanding the dialectic and the tensions about the definition of Dylan in the moment of his transition to rock music, when the

representation of the artist as a folk singer still played a great part in orienting and channeling public perception.

10. Shelton's biography (1986), together with Lee's (2004b) and Bauldie's (1988) reconstructions of the world tour are still the best chronicles of the electric controversy.

THREE

Never Let Me Go

Playfulness and Seriousness in the Rolling Thunder Revue

When Bob Dylan played the Philharmonic Hall in 1964, he joked that he had his Bob Dylan mask on—he was masquerading. More than ten years after that concert, a period during which he helped rewrite the rules of popular music and make rock something serious, or something for a serious audience, he actually added a few nonmetaphorical masks to the ones he had been wearing since the beginning of his career. In 1975, he sometimes had his Richard Nixon mask on, but also a whiteface mask that made him look like a hybrid between a French mime and an American minstrel (there is a hidden tradition of whiteface minstrelsy that goes deep to the heart of American vernacular culture: Strausbaugh 2007, Byrne 2004). Dylan probably played both parts, as one of the main characters of his most theatrical tour, where he took the role of a mysterious Renaldo and let somebody else play "Bob Dylan." This was one of the many puzzling images that could be found in Dylan's four-hour debut as a movie director, *Renaldo and Clara* (Lee 2004a, 89–116), for many an extravagant and redundant exercise in improvisation and intellectualistic cinema that hides a brilliant rockumentary about Dylan's tour of New England in the fall of 1975, the Rolling Thunder Revue.

Just the year before, in January and February 1974, Dylan had reunited with The Band, eight years after the nightly battles of the electric turn. However, the whole experience was not a pleasant one for Dylan, burdened by a mythological narrative about his return to stage and by expectations from audiences and the press. It was right after that tour and moving to New York following a temporary separation from his wife that Dylan started to toy with the idea of a different format, something that could go on forever and that could be "like a circus"—as he told ex-Byrd Roger McGuinn, who would join Dylan's caravan in 1975 (Griffin 2010, 34–35). To some extent, visually and ideologically the first leg of the Rolling Thunder Revue (there would be another one in the spring of 1976) was indeed an experiment designed to bring together the perceived freedom of a circus, its cast of typical and marginal characters, and the transgression from social pressures that an itinerant life could provide. It was as if Dylan and his fellow travelers could realize the fantasy that he had often put into words when he fabricated his biography as a hobo, who had run away from home and was adopted by the world of the circus and the traveling show.

The circus, the masks, and the programmatic outsiderness from the rock world that Dylan was seemingly pursuing with the Rolling Thunder Revue have been extensively discussed by biographers (Shelton 1986, 450–475; Sounes 2001, 255–305; but Sloman 2002, originally published in 1978, is still the best firsthand account). They are also well documented on record (*Hard Rain* and the *Bootleg Series Vol. 5,* as well as a good many bootleg recordings) and in movies like *Renaldo and Clara,* the televised *Hard Rain* special, and the unreleased *Live at the Warehouse*; however, an investigation of the cultural dynamics at work in the Rolling Thunder Revue has been barely attempted. Dylan's idea of a circus, however extemporaneous in its formulation, reveals indeed (and points to) the complexity of the work that he was doing during those years in order to redefine his role as an artist in the context of a high and renewed visibility that he had probably not attained since the mid-1960s. The circus is a strange cultural object, being situated both at the margins of society and as one of its necessary complements. In popular imagination, it provides an outer place for the transition from seriousness to play, from control to freedom. It is, in other words, a territory for a controlled exploration of the margins, for the reversal of social hierarchies, and for the display of outsiderness in such a way that it cannot become a threat to the established orderliness of social relations. The circus, thus, belongs to all those vernacular forms that create pressure from below and outside, producing their ideas about "community" and simultaneously their own nostalgic look at community, the dream of more immediate social relations. This immediateness is probably what attracted Dylan.

Like many other vernacular forms, the circus is a social site of creativity and detachment from societal norms, and it belongs to the wide class of cultural phenomena that prescribe a momentary relaxation from social obligations and expectations. Only in the circus and in akin cultural forms like the carnival, the fool and the freak can become protagonists, irony the general tone of expression. Because they open such a risky space of creativity, reversal, and rebellion, which are often ritualized in marginal behaviors, they cannot go on forever, lest their disruptive power mine the foundations of "normality" upon which society rests. If they have to become permanent characteristics of society, they need to be segregated in specific times, or institutionalized, that is, become subject to rules that make them normal and accepted and inhabited by professionalized characters. As much as the circus stands as a metaphor for personal freedom and an escape from social bonds, it is also a domesticated metaphor where there is always a dialectic between creativity and constraint.

In this process "play" becomes "serious." The "serious"—as opposed to "playful," circus-like—liminality that we find in the whole experience of the Rolling Thunder Revue, with Dylan distancing himself both from his life and from the formats that had been created around the presentation of rock music on stage in the 1970s, is a fundamental component of Dylan's re-creation of his own authenticity in the mid-1970s.

The circus articulates them in what literary theorist Peter Brooks (1976, ix) has characterized as "modes of excess" that involve both the actors' melodramatic presentation (their gestures, their movements, their tones of expression) and the general scripts that govern performance, not as residual elements but as driving forces. Expressive and representational excesses seem to be useful keys in understanding the Rolling Thunder Revue, because they are forms of distancing the artist's stage presentation from ordinary "realism," the idea that "being" is a more fundamental element of performance than "doing" and "showing doing" (Auslander 2004, 6). A musical performance rests on a sort of tacit agreement about an illusion that what we witness on stage is the unmediated self of the artist, and the more the discourse on authenticity has contributed to shape the public image of the artist, the more we are inclined to bypass all the performative artifices that artists use to present their image, their efforts to produce a convincing "characterization" (Auslander 2004). In other words, artists are supposed to act "naturally" in order to create the impression that their authentic self is presented on stage, and this process is all the more evident in those cases in which a charismatic narrative (like the one that has affected Dylan in his career) has contributed to the artist's detachment from the "ordinary" consumption of music as a commodity.

In a sense, the charismatic narrative that had been constructed around Dylan was a fundamental asset that he could exploit in order to advance claims about artistic autonomy and originality as markers of authenticity. As the object of a charismatic narrative, which portrayed him as the source of his own authenticity, Dylan had the opportunity to move outside and against the constraints imposed on him by the institutional field in which he was working. He was seen, in other words, as the source of an autonomous social power, where individual creativity was a crucial trait that he could exploit without many of the filters that were perceived to harm other performers' efforts to become "original." The Rolling Thunder Revue and the Gospel Tour, which I will analyze in the next chapter, relied on this representational trait that constructed Dylan as somebody who was rightly entitled to make his own moves, and in some regards this autonomy was praised both by audiences and other reputational entrepreneurs. These representations reinforce Dylan's perceived charisma, valuing the unmediated relationship among his figure, his work, and his audiences, a trait that he exploited in diverging ways both in the Rolling Thunder (a moment of deep affiliation with the audience, produced in accord with available and powerful representations of Bob Dylan and his authenticity) and in his religious, "born-again" music, when the charismatic narrative was enacted once again in an unexpected career move that meant a disaffiliation between Dylan and his audience. In both cases, Dylan was positioning his work on a spectrum of expressive possibilities that articulated with different accents the playful and the serious. While immersed in this attempt, he was playing with performative genres and with archetypes of performance (like the trickster and the prophet) that were represented in unbalanced ways in the two tours I will consider. Yet, although the Rolling Thunder Revue succeeded in bringing together seriousness and play, the asymmetry created in the Gospel Tour—where a different kind of "seriousness" was embodied by the artist, led to Dylan's fall and the reversal of the charismatic narrative with which he had been associated.

Dylan's Masks

When one considers the first leg of the Rolling Thunder Revue, it is difficult to discriminate between the original vision of the traveling circus that Dylan envisioned and the transformations it was subjected to once Dylan embarked upon the scripting and shooting of *Renaldo and Clara*. For sure, ideas for the movie shaped Dylan's persona on stage. *Renaldo and Clara* (of which I cannot provide a full synopsis or overview here) falls somewhere between Dylan's attempt to deconstruct the narrative foundations of cinema and an exercise in postmodernist, nouvelle vague bricolage. Its set of characters is a citationist translation of Marcel Carné's 1940s masterpiece *Les enfants du paradis* (*Children of Paradise*), and Dylan's Renaldo is modeled after the mime Baptiste, who is one of the main protagonists of Carné's account of life, anguish, unrequited love, and theater in the 1830s. There are similarities between the whiteface Dylan and the whiteface Baptiste, both in terms of the visual effect that a painted face brings and in thematic terms, because both *Renaldo and Clara* and *Children of Paradise* are constructed around the protagonist's relationship with a mysterious "woman in white." The cohort of side characters makes Dylan's movie a modernized-Americanized version of Carné's movie (minus narrative consistency).[1]

If one wants to make sense of the various meanings of Bob Dylan during the first leg of the Rolling Thunder Revue, which was also the time the crew worked on *Renaldo and*

Clara, the tensions that emerge within Dylan's whiteface persona provide an excellent starting point. Not only was the mask a powerful visual element that became central to Dylan's performance, it was also in the whiteface mask that the two cultural traditions to which Dylan was referring (playful lowbrow circus and serious highbrow cinema) condensed and clashed.

Masks serve a double function: they attract attention as much as they hide those who wear them. They are thus peculiar objects that enter an identity game, allowing questions to arise about the motives, the meanings, and the place that the artist holds while wearing the mask. In some sense, they point to a persona different from the artist, and at the same time they make the artist the focus of questions about his reasons for engaging himself in this play of identities.

Dylan's masks were revealed an hour or so after the beginning of the show, which was scripted in such a way as to create anticipation and to signal the Revue's communitarian mood. Individual band members, followed by Bobby Neuwirth and Ronee Blakley (then at the peak of her fame, following her participation in Robert Altman's *Nashville*) sang one or two songs each. Then, Ramblin' Jack Elliott (a link to the hobo tradition via his personal relationship with Woody Guthrie) was on stage for four songs, right before Dylan's first set. Without any further announcement, Bobby Neuwirth (who was the real master of ceremonies during the first leg of the Rolling Thunder) appeared with an acoustic guitar. An unrecognizable character joins him, while the first chords of "When I Paint My Masterpiece" lead into Dylan and Neuwirth's vigorous rendition of the song. On the debut night in Plymouth (October 30, 1975), Neuwirth just says, "here's an old friend," and then Dylan and he struggle to harmonize. "Masterpiece" would be the standard opener for the rest of the thirty-one-date tour. The song, beginning with its title, was an aesthetic statement quite different from the songs that Dylan had chosen to open with in 1974 with The Band: "Hero Blues" ("You need a different kind of man, babe, You need Napoleon Bonaparte") and then "Most Likely You Go Your Way and I Go Mine," two songs that give a nod to the audience and reclaim the singer's autonomy from their expectations.

Yet, for the whole first leg of the Rolling Thunder, the song about the audience was not played late in the set. The song was a reworked electric arrangement of "It Ain't Me, Babe," and it was a song that always deserved special attention, because it was while singing it that Dylan revealed his game of masks to the public. Unfortunately, the officially released *Bootleg Series* that documents the 1975 Rolling Thunder Revue misses the powerful narrative that Dylan performed on stage, with an invitation to the audience to wait and see, because, "Someday, everything is gonna be diff'rent, When I paint my masterpiece." The *Bootleg Series Vol. 5* (a collection of performances taken from different shows and, as such, not entirely representative of the structure of Dylan's set, or of the relationship it had with other artists' presentations) starts with an excellent version of "Tonight I'll Be Staying Here with You" (which was added to the setlist much later in the tour and was never an opener), a joyous performance that suggests complicity both with the occasional lover Dylan sings to and about and with the audience, to which the meaning of the song can be metaphorically extended. Indeed, a widely circulated bootleg makes this reference explicit: *Get Ready! Tonight Bob Will Be Staying Here with You.*

Just as "Tonight I'll Be Staying Here with You" is an invitation to the audience, "It Ain't Me, Babe" is a declaration of autonomy, a song that Dylan has often chosen as a tender closer to his shows (especially during some phases of the Never Ending Tour). In the Rolling Thunder Revue, coupled with an aesthetic statement about art and creation, like "When I Paint My Masterpiece," the song—and its performance, including Dylan's display of his "self" on stage—works with the familiar themes of Dylan's image and his relationship with the audience. It was not the first time "It Ain't Me, Babe" served that function. It was played during the electric tour with The Hawks in 1965, only to be abandoned after the American leg. But during the Rolling Thunder Revue, Dylan's declaration of independence was even more accentuated. In Forest Hills 1965, the audience responded half-angrily to the refrain, the catchy "no, no, no, it ain't me, babe," a phrase that communicated distance and disengagement in both directions. During the Rolling Thunder, Dylan's right to electrify the song was never called into question. There are no doubts that this arrangement and Dylan's singing work—it was often a highlight of the show, as was the electronic version of "The Lonesome Death of Hattie Carroll," another song that would have been met with catcalls in 1965. Dylan's dramatic abilities to inhabit the songs he sings are revealed in his performance of "It Ain't Me, Babe," when he occasionally stresses the word *you* in the line, "I'm not the one you want babe." In a song that is constructed around the opposition between I/me and you, the monologue that Dylan addresses to his audience makes clear from the very beginning where he stands and where he'd like his audience to stand. Engaging as it is, effective and loose (especially in the first concerts, when the band has not yet jelled, and Dylan does the most work with his voice and phrasing), "It Ain't Me, Babe" reinforces Dylan's declaration of autonomy. The audience stands outside the community Dylan wants to create, and the presentation of autonomy is more important than the invitation for the audience to take part in this community.

The audience is also presented with the usual, kaleidoscopic Dylan, even more so during the Rolling Thunder Revue, when the singer is hidden behind two masks that give, in the space of two songs, an idea of Dylan's embodiment of Arthur Rimbaud's motto, "I is another." Dylan starts his set wearing a Richard Nixon mask, which makes him unrecognizable to the audience (in a couple of cases, somebody shouts, "It's Dylan," but not before he begins to sing). As he sings "It Ain't Me, Babe" he takes the Nixon mask off (before the harmonica break), only to reveal that he is painted with white, theatrical makeup. At one point an audience member asks him why he is in whiteface. "The meaning is in the words," Dylan replies (Kokay 2003). This reversal of the original, filmic inspiration (the mime who does not speak becomes an actor whose only point of reference is in words) makes Dylan closer to the clown and the trickster, who are programmatically designed to speak forbidden truths while invoking laughter. Yet, even this ideal is quite far from Dylan's presentation of the artist on stage, because the image of the trickster remains in the background (still in the space of the circus to which it belongs, though), and Dylan explores the "seriousness" of music and performance on stage, with first sets that feature his apocalyptic "A Hard Rain's A-Gonna Fall" and the most theatrical song of the Rolling Thunder, the then-unreleased "Isis," which Dylan used to sing without his guitar, waving

his hands in a way that mimicked the most heated moments of the 1966 tour.

This dialectic between Dylan's projected seriousness and
the playful circus-like format in which it was embedded
needs further consideration, because it highlights once more
the fundamental traits of the construction of Dylan's authenticity. In a sense, the first leg of the Rolling Thunder Revue
was a revivalist project, informed by notions of authenticity
that Dylan had explored and learned about in his first few
years in New York and that—despite the electric frenzy of
his rise to rock-stardom in 1965 and 1966—he had never
abandoned, even in his most lackluster adventures in music
for *Self Portrait.* The problem lies in the peculiar configuration
of hard-core authenticity that Dylan seemed to be seeking
during the Rolling Thunder Revue and the way it expressed
the musical margins that are a fundamental part of Dylan's
approach to music and performing. It was a brave move beyond the rock culture and the superstar's centrality in the
1970s (in visual and performative, if not strictly musical,
terms). But how did the elements that Dylan kept from rock
merge with the circus-like experience of the Rolling Thunder
Revue? To answer that question, one has to consider the
long waves of influences (musical as well as performative)
the folk revival had well into the 1970s.[2]

The Rolling Thunder Revue as a
Revivalist Memory Project

During the first leg of the Rolling Thunder Revue, Dylan usually played three sets, two with Guam (with the occasional
solo acoustic number that opened his third set) and a set with
Joan Baez, in which they reenacted memories of their joint
tours and guest appearances in the first half of the 1960s.
Songwriter and playwright Jacques Levy, with whom Dylan
collaborated at the time and who scripted the shows, chose
a very theatrical entrance for those shows that took place
in smaller venues, with Dylan and Baez playing behind the
stage curtain, which was lifted only after they had begun to
sing. To increase the dramatic effect, Baez and Dylan sometimes looked like twins, sharing the microphone and dressed
in similar ways, white makeup included. They always opened

with one of Dylan's songs from the folk years, either "Blowin' in the Wind" or "The Times They Are A-Changin'," with the occasional performance of the traditional "The Water Is Wide." With the exception of Johnny Ace's "Never Let Me Go" and the exploration of some of Dylan's post-incident songs (like "I Dreamed I Saw Saint Augustine" and "I Shall Be Released," incidentally songs that belong to Dylan's exploration of a new palette of American roots in the *Basement Tapes/John Wesley Harding* period), their set could have come straight out of the 1964 Newport Folk Festival. It represented the strong element of the centrality of the visions of performing authenticity and community that Dylan and Baez had learned during the folk revival.

Visual and musical links to the folk revival abounded. In the original flyer of the tour, the three headliners were Dylan, Baez, and Ramblin' Jack Elliott (with Bob Neuwirth listed in the flyer as well), three singers who indeed represented the revival, especially its urban dimension and the enactment of outsiderness that the urban folk revival often allowed its members. Other artists in the Rolling Thunder (like Roger McGuinn and Joni Mitchell) came from the same milieu. They were, thus, accustomed to the communitarian idea of making music together, which was very well present in Dylan's mind when he originally started to think about the tour, and which he had seen again in the lively context of the Village scene in the mid-1970s, when many of those artists who had left the revival for rock were discovering their folk roots for a second time. Indeed, a few features made the Rolling Thunder shows in 1975 (1976 would be another matter, affected both by personal disenchantment and a more commercial logic) a reenactment of a revivalist show, similar to those hootenannies that had been the original context out of which Dylan emerged as a folk artist: They usually lasted about four hours, with multiple performers on stage, and with big names singing one or two songs (as was the case for McGuinn). There was room for guest artists (like Joni Mitchell, who later joined the tour, Arlo Guthrie, or Gordon Lightfoot) and impromptu appearances on stage. Traditional songs were often performed, usually by Jack Elliott, Dylan, and Baez; finally, there was a hootenanny-like performance to close the show, a significant reprise of Woody Guthrie's "This Land Is Your Land," in the year that led to the Bicentennial celebrations, sung by all the main acts of the show (and with everybody else joining in for the chorus).

If Dylan's original idea was to stage a show that brought community back to rock stardom, then his references (the one he knew well) could only come from the vision of the folk revival with which he had been socialized and in which even the vernacular forms that he wanted the Rolling Thunder to look like had been accepted. The idea of the circus and the traveling show, indeed, had been filtered through the experience of the revival and its attention to the preservation of cultural forms coming from the people. Thus, the circus-like authenticity that Dylan sought to recreate was in line with the modernized vision of the circus as a form of vernacular art, where the marginal authenticity of "the people" came into being. If this worked from the aesthetic point of view, it also had implications for the construction of the vision of the artist that Dylan was eager to embody during the first leg of the Rolling Thunder. The Rolling Thunder represents Dylan's first attempt to work with the hybridization of genres during his shows, and not only in his records. What had left Dylan dissatisfied with the 1974 tour (and later with the 1978 tour) was probably the professionalization of musical experience and the absence of moments of free-flowing expression, an aspect of the institutionalization of rock that had become prominent in the 1970s.

In both cases, Dylan reacted in similar ways, working on the genre of performance, creating a show as a hybrid, and defining a wider space for the memory of American popular music. This vision has been with him ever since, whether it has taken the form of the circus, the witnessing of the Gospel in the tours that followed his conversion, or the memory projects that have characterized the Never Ending Tour. It is an ongoing dialogue with American traditions that involves Dylan at his best, but in any case distant and distinct from the narratives of rock that have been built around him (indeed, when Dylan has gone "rock" in the past thirty years, the result has often been questionable, forced as he has been to enact a stereotyped image of Bob Dylan). But it is also a dialogue that takes authenticity as a central concern, especially the hard-core vision of authenticity that I have illustrated in the previous chapters. If this version of authenticity is the key aspect in understanding Dylan's attempts to construct his reputation among his audiences, it must also be noted that hard-core performers usually move from the periphery, making a claim about the legitimacy of musical forms that predate the commercialization and commodification of rock music and, on the contrary, explore both its limits and its borders, where other forms of music (country, the blues, and folk songs) have fallen. They stand, in other words, outside of boundaries, or on the demarcation line between mainstream stardom (which Dylan touched in the mid-1970s) and marginal projects that deal with the expression of their outsiderness, the only viable way to create authenticity and originality.

The Rolling Thunder Revue seems to be no exception in this sense, because it shares fundamental traits with many other projects building "Bob Dylan" from the margins and the peripheries of mainstream American popular culture. What is peculiar about the experience of the Rolling Thunder, though, are the performative ideas of community that Dylan embodied and the collective representations of vernacular forms (circuses, carnivals, and traveling shows) that were used to script, stage, and perform the shows.

The traveling show—especially the circus as one of the central genres in American popular spectacles—has traditionally been a site of the exchange between impoverished theatrical form (if and when considered from the perspective of high culture) and bottom-up cultural repertoires of the subaltern classes. In the context of the traveling show, the common ground for this interchange between the lowered high and the genuinely vernacular works in the key integration of play, irony, and performance. It belongs to what play theorist Brian Sutton-Smith has identified as a "rhetoric of the imaginary" (Sutton-Smith 1997) that defies expectations in the audience and that is embodied in the figure of the clown, the trickster, and the con man as central to the ironic and almost carnival-esque tone of performance in the traveling show. These deviant figures are essential because they are the performers of a peripheral authenticity, not sanctioned by cultural institutions other than the ones that come from below, and which belong to a myth of performative deviance, the ability to use irony, the masquerade, and the leveling of social relations as a key to understanding social life but also to promote social change.

The cultural work of the circus is framed with reference to these assumptions, in the professionalized unprofessionalism of the clown and as the embodiment of subaltern skills (like the skill of the juggler, the strength of the weightlifter or amateur boxer, or the comic effect of animals acting like humans) that are commonly reframed in the spectacle. Within this frame, Dylan's efforts were political at a deeper level than his occasional commitment to "causes" like that of Rubin "Hurricane" Carter, which he supported during the first leg of the Rolling Thunder Revue. In a sense, playing with the traditional from the margins was not only Dylan's main attitude to performance, but also his political statement, which was condensed in the idea that being "authentic" implied this kind of attention to genres and memories that came from the periphery of American society, both the periphery represented by tradition and the periphery of the remnants of the counterculture, which were able to make sense of the intellectual and dramaturgical outsiderness of the Rolling Thunder Revue.

The 1960s counterculture, which had taken Dylan simultaneously as its idol and its creator, aligned to the deeper narratives of the leisure-like and horizontal character of the Rolling Thunder Revue. Accordingly, Dylan's reputation grew because the performer brought on stage a visible impression of that community-like organization on which the counterculture itself had based its political and ideological claims. Quite ironically, thus, Dylan was perceived as an artist who was back in his role as representative of that counterculture in the very moment that his show, by relying on older and almost transhistorical narratives about the reversal of social relations and the affirmation of their horizontality, hinted at the nonspecific and nonrevolutionary nature of the claims coming from his audience. If that was a misunderstanding, then it was an effective way to construct both the image of Dylan as rooted in the culture of his time and an image of Dylan as an entrepreneur able to work with a genre that could belong to a distant past and tradition that had its roots in the nineteenth century.

Yet this whole process reveals both the plurality and the polysemy of the cultural practices associated with the transformation of Dylan's image and role in the mid-1970s. The Rolling Thunder Revue, to some extent, was an exercise in the performance of polysemy, in the definition of alternative paths that spoke simultaneously about the artist, the show, the audience, and the whole set of different traditional or traditionalized elements they could use in order to make sense of Dylan as a performer and as an artist. The whole tour, therefore, generated a feeling of anachronism, despite all its references, stylistic and not, to the genre of rock that the musicians were expressing on stage. The Rolling Thunder was rather the first extensive instance where Dylan tried to achieve a public and performative reconciliation with the tradition coming from the folk revival and his present status as rock musician. Dylan's image was crafted, and simultaneously received, in this dialogue between past and present, which tried to get rid of the constraints imposed by the institutionalized concept of the "rock concert" as it had been shaped since the mid-1960s. Memory, in this sense, worked both as a resource and as a fragmented reference, proposed by the artist as an extra-performative reference, useful for making sense of the whole project of the tour.

However, rock and the other memories that Dylan was enacting from outside of the rock tradition and closer to the revivalists' vision of authenticity were the two poles of an opposition that had to be reconciled on stage. The Rolling Thunder Revue, thus, simultaneously provided the opportunity to work with different genres and the opportunity for the public to see the dilemmas involved in the reconciliation of rock and other cultural frameworks. Dylan was performing his hits and other old songs, singing duets with Neuwirth and Baez, and—at the same time—reproducing the notions of individualism that he had espoused when he abandoned the revival.

The Artist as Individual in the Rolling Thunder Revue

This dialectic interaction between individualism and the values coming from a more collective vision of art and musical work has always constituted a crucial axis for interpreting Dylan's role as an artist. It has resulted in conflicting representations that emphasize Dylan's historical role as a "spokesman" (embedding his artistic reputation in a

wider narrative that is—at its roots—highly collectivistic)
or his ability to distance himself from a series of collectives
—whether they be social movements, audiences, or communities of artists that are supposed to share the same
basic assumptions about music, its social place, and its
means of performance. These representations—which have
contributed to the multivocal image of Bob Dylan over the
past fifty years—have gained more and more strength as
Dylan's figure as a star became more and more autonomous
from the original circumstances of its social production in
the 1960s. He has often been perceived as a musician able
to produce a condensation of the spirit of the times in his
work and figure, while standing, however, in an autonomous
position, seemingly not touched by the logic of production
that governs popular music. This has been the long-term
effect, in representational terms, of Dylan's inclusion
among "authentic" singer-songwriters in the 1960s, when
his career trajectory was rationalized and justified in terms
of a progressive and liberating narrative, moving from the
constraints of the collectivistic imposition of political values
coming from the folk revival to a more individualistic stance
synthesized by the two major factors that Dylan worked in
the field of popular music, the first by creating a new territory for songwriting and the second by matching this newly
branded "politics of style" with electric rock. Individual and
collective interpretations of Dylan's work have often been
effective in constraining representations, but they also have
served as powerful means of generating expectations about a
social role that Dylan is assumed to play beyond the domain
of popular music.

Whether he is interpreted publicly as the one and only
source of his own artistic moves or he is expected to act and
perform as the symbol for wider social values translated into
music, Dylan as an individual performing artist has always
been evaluated at the intersection of multiple discourses that
have defined his role for the wider audience and which, in
turn, have been filtered through the public actions of Dylan
himself. Dylan's perceived authenticity has served to keep
together the two poles of individualism and collectivism,
though not without tensions and movements that have produced at various times in his career an unbalanced discourse
about whether he stood on the individualistic side or was

willing to accept the political and aesthetic constraints of a collectivistic approach to music-making.

The artist is also responsible for some of the changes in the public representation of "Bob Dylan," as evidenced by Dylan's shape-shifting attitude. The stage is one of the most relevant settings—sometimes, the exclusive setting—for presenting the dominance of one or the other of the two sides to the public. The Rolling Thunder Revue was no exception, but it relied more subtly on the representational elements of Dylan's perceived autonomy in shaping his relationship with the audience and in supporting his perceived difference as a rock star able to transcend the limits imposed by the cultural industry. Both individualism and collectivism, as core values attached to performing music, seem to serve as background representations that can be exploited in an attempt to carry Dylan's image beyond the routine arrangement and working procedures of the music industry. This promotes his status as an artist outside the norm, who works in a social space that seems to have its only source of legitimation in the artist himself.

Dylan's—which is essential to understanding his star image—consists of socially constructed representations that are used to support claims about artistic authenticity and about Dylan's position both within and outside the domain of popular music. The performance of music ensures visibility of the artist's efforts to position himself in accordance with the available representations constructed about his authenticity. In many cases, indeed, performance is scripted in such a way that it relies on these images of authenticity and is aimed at reinforcing them. In other words, the core characteristics of Dylan's authenticity can be broadcast to the audience and witnessed.

Both the first and the second leg of the Rolling Thunder Revue were attempts to project the kind of marginal authenticity that Dylan had previously explored. Both were intended—in their representations, format of performance, and scripts—as occasions for distancing Dylan from the institutionalized format for the presentation of rock stardom that he had experienced in the past and which had left him unsatisfied. Yet, although they were embedded in the exploration of circus-like marginality, in the aesthetic recreation of a community of performers, and in the revivalist projects

I have discussed, the two legs of the tour stand in stark contrast of one another, because they articulated two radically opposed visions of the way Dylan could represent the role of the individual artist—as bearer of a communitarian approach to making music, or as an actor who could reclaim and perform his subjectivity while on stage.

Although Dylan used the same title for both legs of the Rolling Thunder tour, they were two different musical projects and two different musical proposals, centered performatively on Dylan's most recent albums. Whereas the first leg showcased new songs from *Desire* (which have often been described as Dylan's songs of redemption: Witting 2002), the second leg moved back to the very bitter lyrics of *Blood on the Tracks*. In the first leg, most of the shows featured Dylan on stage playing in whiteface his fictional character Renaldo, from *Renaldo and Clara*. Without the need to shoot the movie, Dylan adopted a different—and to some extent more threatening—stage persona, from the wandering gipsy and the nouvelle vague mime he had impersonated in the fall. Similarly, the performances of the songs from *Blood on the Tracks* were characterized by an explicit urgency that was lacking in the shows in the fall leg. Paul Williams has noted, convincingly, that the second leg of the Rolling Thunder Revue sounded like "*Blood on the Tracks*, take three" (Williams 1994, 83; after the first recordings of the songs in New York and the subsequent and hurried changes he made in Minnesota in December 1974; for a history of those sessions see Gill and Odegard 2005). The prominence that Dylan gave to this record stands out as a kind of performed autobiography. The personal Dylan that many commentators saw in Rolling Thunder 1976 was at the expense of the more collective and nonindividualized version of the artist that had been seen in the fall. Again, it was performance that changed the image of the artist presented to the audience.

The second Rolling Thunder Revue was less infused with the revivalist approach to authenticity that had informed the first leg. It turned out to be a more conservative attempt at staging Dylan's own authenticity, in a movement from the collective to the individual that resembled Dylan's transition in the 1960s. In a very similar way, Dylan was presenting himself as the spokesman of his own subjectivity, a project whose expression *Blood on the Tracks* allowed with its songs of hate, love, and abandonment, which were captured in the videos of the *Live at the Warehouse* and *Hard Rain* concerts. Except for "Meet Me in the Morning" and "Buckets of Rain," all the songs from the album were played during the spring leg, including a one-off performance of "Lily Rosemary and the Jack of Hearts" (Salt Lake City; there is no known recording of this concert), a melodically captivating version of "You're Gonna Make Me Lonesome When You Go," a radically rewritten "If You See Her Say Hello," and what was to become the focal point of the shows, "Idiot Wind."

Dylan's rearranged version of "Idiot Wind" drew its strength in and from performance, not only as a personal statement but also as a means to present the artists' individual character, a vision suggested by the close-up, almost permanent image of Dylan's face that was used in *Hard Rain* when he sang "Idiot Wind." Whereas in *Renaldo and Clara* this filmic trick often worked as a means to show Dylan's masks and Chaplin-esque moves, in the *Hard Rain* TV special, it contributed to the detachment of the artist —portrayed as an individual—from the collective band to which he belonged, which was for the most part audible but not visible. These differences sum up the different moods and visions that ultimately characterized the two legs of the Rolling Thunder Revue.

The two legs of the Rolling Thunder Revue thus offered the public a contradiction, by articulating a dialectic between the individual and the collective (and between two different conceptions of the subjectivity of the artist) that is expressed through public action and performance. The Rolling Thunder Revue worked within this contradiction, neither able nor willing to solve it, and the two legs of the tour stand as occasions where performance articulated the valence and the salience of the two visions of the artist. It is in the Rolling Thunder Revue that we can witness a shift from the playfulness of performance toward its serious tone, highlighted by Dylan's songs and parallel moves from the collective toward the individual and the individualized character of many of his performances, even when he was being backed up by the band. In a sense, this also meant the temporary rejection of the ideals of playful complicity that Dylan had adopted, because they could not be publicly exploited when Dylan shifted his strategy for presenting the artist. It was a radical individualism that went so far as to present on stage songs that touched what many have perceived to be Dylan's deepest feelings. This tension between the two Dylans, who inhabited in different ways the two legs of the Rolling Thunder Revue, reworked in important ways the original idea of the circus as well as the artist's ability to exploit deep themes in the vernacular culture of American popular music.

A double-sided authenticity was constructed around the expression of the personal side of Dylan's work and the side that was more centered on deep cultural elements, the core of what Greil Marcus has called the "invisible Republic." If we take a look at the songs Dylan played on stage in the band, especially the songs that were not recorded or composed in the mid-1970s, we see a shift toward the Dylan of the Basement Tapes, John Wesley Harding, and *Nashville Skyline*. This is even more evident when compared with his nostalgia-driven tour with The Band.

This seems to be the long-lasting legacy of the Dylan who tried to find a new ground for expression in the Rolling Thunder Revue. The songs Dylan played in 1975 and 1976 can make sense only if we stay true to the idea of the circus as the presentation of marginality and as the occasion to work concretely on the visions of Dylan as an individual, which have accompanied his artistic trajectory, most notably the two related and highly individualistic figures of the trickster and the prophet, representing the playful and the serious, respectively.

Dylan's Subjectivity as Trickster and Prophet

Since his abandonment of the folk revival, Dylan's authenticity has always been perceived as the outcome of an individualistic approach to being authentic, which has worked even when Dylan has seemed more inclined to refer aesthetically to the collectivistic values of folk music and the ideology of sociality it expresses. Oftentimes, Dylan could be perceived as authentic only as long as he could project to the public this multidimensionality and his ability to change as if they were highly personal and individual traits, almost naturally present in the artist and clear markers of his talent. Quite ironically, what has always been expected from Dylan is that he could take unexpected turns, thus providing an image that placed him simultaneously in a field where he was able to follow the rules and against a much more romantic background where the originality of creation played a crucial role in the definition of his authenticity. It is no surprise, then, that Dylan has often been described in parallel with many liminal figures of Western culture, from the shape-shifting Proteus to the prophet and the trickster.

Stephen Scobie has probably been the most acute interpreter of the two faces that Dylan, like the Latin god Janus, has worn all his life and which have defined the projection of his work to the public. Certainly Dylan was a prophet (although a reluctant one, appointed by others) during his brief period of commitment to topical songwriting, when he embodied the spirit of the times by singing words that were as ancient as the Bible and as clean-cut as those coming from a Puritan riding on the *Mayflower* (an image he played with in "Bob Dylan's 115th Dream"). And he prophesied —as we shall see in the next chapter—when he went off the trail of rock stardom to find Jesus in 1979. If the prophet stands on the side of promise and points his finger to the future, the trickster is the creator that, by force of his creativity, disrupts stability (Scobie 2003, 31). Or, as Charles Lemert has argued in his book on the master-trickster of the 1960s (probably even more than Dylan)—Muhammad Ali—"surprise, if not quite irony, is the trickster's potion" (Lemert 2003, 35), which he uses to pull himself and the Other that he embodies out of the margins of society straight to a center to which he does not ultimately belong. Both the trickster and the prophet share this liminal quality (Hyde 1998; Scobie 2003, 32; Turner 1969). Yet, Lemert is right in pointing out that the trickster takes advantage from an ironic vision of liminality itself. He can make a fool of himself as easily as he can denounce others without restraint. In other words, he "plays," and in this sense he is akin to and simultaneously distant from the prophet (the two figures are usually kept distinct, and this distinction is most prominent in the differences between the figure of Jesus Christ in the canonical gospels and in the apocryphal tradition). The prophet works within the liminal, he promises a structured and stable future; he disrupts the present but seeks order in the future. The trickster disrupts as a form of art for art itself, or, in anthropologist Victor Turner's words, his actions are less liminal than *liminoid*: "One works at the liminal, one plays with the liminoid" (Turner 1982, 55). Most modern-day aesthetic and recreational activity, free of the constraints of religious ritual, belongs more to the liminoid rather than to the liminal—our world is characterized by activities that resemble rituals but are not exactly like them, because they introduce an element of recreation and disengagement from the seriousness of everyday life: plays, games, concerts, sports, and a wide range of secular celebrations. So do the figures that perform them; they are playful even when they try to be serious, but—in turn—seriousness never fails to find its way into their attempts to play their tricks and games.

Performances, whether in theaters, concert halls, or sports arenas, or in the circus for that matter, always bring in this playful element. Performance shares with ritual the pressure to achieve a state of community, and it shares with play the fact that the steps that lead toward community are not fixed, but are able to be creatively produced by those who engage in playful activity. I argue that artistic creation, especially that which takes place within the performing arts, often takes this shape, where there is something obligatory (a script, the pressure to connect to the audience) but also a great deal of free-form, unexpected, and contingent creation, which contributes to the definition of the status of the artist. The role of the individual comes back vehemently as a source of art, but what has to be noted here is that these are still social, cultural, and interactional processes: one needs to know how the liminoid and the ritual-like work, in order to play with them and their emergent rules.

This ability to work within rules, while at the same time stretching them, is often misrecognized as a sign of an artist's originality. Marshall, in his careful reconstruction of Dylan's star-status and the turns it has had since his debut, argues adamantly that "it is important not to over-sociologize: the star still has some power to shape their public meaning although it is less than conventionally presented.... What stars themselves actually do is important for reinforcing or contradicting audience beliefs, for chipping away at the boundaries of their meaning" (Marshall 2007, 187). Quite true, if we hold that the artist is shaped exclusively by social structures (and apparatuses of production and ideological reproduction) that pressure from outside and above. Yet, all these strategies of re-creation (and in Dylan's case, of shape-shifting) must rely on available *cultural structures* that constitute the boundaries and the tools that the artist can use to work on his meaning and on the expectations of the audience. However loose, even the most free-form phenomenon is projected against the background of culture, and it could not be understood at all if it were not for these structures that enhance both understanding and creation.

In other words, the artist plays an autonomous role (relatively speaking, as his image always has to be broadcast to a public that in turn has to evaluate him, a collective dimension of artistic activity that sociologist Howard Becker has described effectively: Becker 1982), when he is able to work —and play—within those boundaries, and not outside them, lest his work be dismissed as irrelevant or "not artistic." However, these paths are programmatically not fixed, and there is always great room for individual agency, particularly when it comes from and works within the margins provided by liminoid forms of performance. It is in those forms that the artist is likely to experience the largest freedom of expression. This argument is consistent—as we shall see—with Dylan's enactment of authenticity, an authenticity that has been constructed and recognized by taking cultural peripheries as the starting point for movement toward the center: from folk to rock, and once rock had been established, from the many forms of vernacular culture, inhabited by tricksters, clowns, outlaws, and outsiders, to the center of rock, where Dylan's discourse about authenticity has been a trick in itself, claiming legitimacy for all those musical forms (country, gospel, bluegrass) that rock had seemed to bury in the past, the moment it affirmed itself as a radical origin of contemporary popular music.

From this point of view, the Rolling Thunder Revue was a deliberate attempt to work on Dylan's masks in such a way that they added to his authenticity in aesthetic, musical, and even intellectual terms. At the same time, the focus on community that was one of the tour's core values seems to have served as the first intentional attempt, on Dylan's part, to distance himself from the ideology of stardom that had been attached to him (and through which he had been interpreted) in the years of his rise to fame, an ideology that later turned into a mystic vision of Dylan's invisibility during the years of his semiretirement. Returning to live music in 1974, Dylan probably found no way to express the vision of authenticity that defined his figure within the constraints imposed by a largely changing rock culture. The Rolling Thunder, then, stood out as the attempt to redefine those rules while creating an autonomous space for the artist. "Autonomy," indeed, is a fundamental trait of Dylan's authenticity, and in the Rolling Thunder, in its format and even in its performative choices, we can witness how it worked as a means to create a different vision of Bob Dylan, able to defy expectations and consolidated representations. What is important, in this sense, is how these ideas about marginality, authenticity, and the artist's subjectivity have contributed to shape not only Dylan's work in the nearly forty years that followed the Rolling Thunder, but also how they have created performance as the environment where Dylan not only presents himself on stage, but also as the key moment when the public is exposed to and called to evaluate "Bob Dylan."

Conclusions

In this chapter, I have focused on the contradictions that were worked out in Dylan's tours in the mid-1970s, and I have tried to make explicit a constellation of themes and problems that gave shape to the two different projects of the Rolling Thunder Revue. It is indeed quite surprising that so much beyond music found its way in the Rolling Thunder Revue and its project of playing with vernacular genres, closing the gap between performance in rock and much older forms of performance that had their roots in theater and the vernacular tradition. Dylan's Rolling Thunder in 1975 and 1976 consisted of a set of performances that tried to reach a synthesis between a set of oppositions (rock/theater, serious/playful, prophet/trickster, individual/collective) that have characterized Dylan's career as a whole. The solution that Dylan seemingly found—in intent if not in its results—affected both his presentation on stage and the general tone of his performance. The dimensions of theater and play had never been so present in Dylan's concerts, and they fueled Dylan's detachment from the constraints of expression that regulated rock-stardom in the 1970s.

Quite amazingly, this recreation of the role of the artist took place when Dylan was in his second peak of popularity, following the release of the much-praised *Blood on the Tracks* and a highly successful tour, at least from the commercial point of view. Dylan's response to those pressures was a renewed connection with traditions and with the core authenticity that he found usually in marginal forms. From this point of view, the influence of the Rolling Thunder Revue has lasted well beyond the conclusion of that tour and has shaped Dylan's further attempts to stage his authenticity through intentional genre-work, the commitment to the exploration of cultural memory, and the renovation of the performance of "rock" through the creation of hybrid forms of performance and representation.

This hybridization seems to be less an extemporaneous attempt, and more a defining trait of Dylan's image and artistic reputation, closely connected to the vision of authenticity that has defined Dylan as an artist. Different attitudes to performance, genres, and different projections of the meaning of the artist were presented in a fluid context, in which Dylan tried to play with the constraints of performance and with the deep themes that made it possible. As such, the Rolling Thunder is less an enclosed musical and theatrical project than it is a moment of condensation and re-creation of Dylan's image and authenticity, whose seeds are still present today as Dylan has moved to embody many of the neglected memories of the American musical landscape. Even his least successful attempts, and his most controversial ones, are defined with reference to these ideals, which enhance the artist's attitude toward genres, both as broad cultural references and guidelines for the remaking of an artist as a symbol. As I will illustrate in the next chapter, Dylan's much-debated (and opposed) conversion to Christianity and his controversial project of a "Gospel Tour" are no exceptions. They, too, use the unsafe environment of the stage as the social site in which to play with musical genres, twist their boundaries, and work on "Bob Dylan" as a symbol.

Notes

1. More than thirty years later, *Renaldo and Clara* stands out as an oddity—and a perceived failure—in Dylan's career, revered by fans and scorned by critics as one of the most daring and controversial moves of his career. The best, most concise interpretation of the movie can be found in Dunlap (2005).

2. We can see the rock superstar, a role Dylan problematically played in 1974 with The Band and, in 1978, as one element of an opposition within the culture of authenticity. The rock superstar, as the product of an ideology of rock that puts the system of production at the center, is contrasted with more authentic attempts to work within and against the rules of superstardom, either by producing a populist discourse that connects the star to the people (as in the case of Bruce Springsteen) or an intellectualistic discourse that challenges the boundaries of the field of popular music and produces a claim that the star plays a wider social role.

FOUR

Blessed Be the Name of the Lord

Performing the Conversion during the Gospel Tour

November 2008. The United Palace Theater in Washington Heights, New York, was the perfect venue for the first performance of "Gotta Serve Somebody" in four years. It was a lavish ex-theater turned into a church, with religious banners hanging from the walls of the foyer. Right after the introduction, with its meaningful nod to a Dylan who had "emerged to find Jesus" after "disappearing into a haze of substance abuse," the band took the stage, and a familiar guitar riff, heavy with blues echoes, filled the theater. Then Dylan's voice, so deep and gravelly it might have been Howlin' Wolf's, led the audience into a five-minute tour de force with the familiar words, "You might be an ambassador to England or France, you might like to gamble you might like to dance." As he went on singing, the lyrics became less familiar. Dylan was ad-libbing, bringing to the stage words he had read in the entrance hall: "No matter where you are, or where you been, but you gotta serve Somebody."

These days, when Dylan sings something from his Gospel years, thunderous applause usually signals the audience's approval, because the appearance of one of those songs is a quite rare event. Over the past twenty years, Dylan has never been shy about singing songs that have a strong religious tone, whether they are the old country numbers that have made many nights of his Never Ending Tour special, or one of the recent openers—"Gonna Change My Way of Thinking," another song from *Slow Train Coming,* the first album of his religious trilogy of the late 1970s, early 1980s—which he even sang in Israel in June 2011, in his first concert there in eighteen years. He was careful enough, though, to start the line "Jesus is coming, coming to gather his jewels" a few inches away from the microphone.

When these songs were first presented and performed in public, however, they created a controversy that was equal, if not worse, to the one that arose when Dylan abandoned the folk revival and "went electric." For six months, between November 1979 and May 1980, Dylan embarked on three legs of a "Gospel" tour, where he witnessed his newly found Christian faith and stopped performing any material that was not related to his conversion. Dylan sang and preached, in concerts that can be easily regarded among the finest he has played in his career, and yet he was met with scorn, ridiculed by his audience, and butchered by the critics, eventually losing an important part of his audience. It was a complete reversal of the trajectory that Dylan had experienced during the electric turn. Whereas in this latter case, Dylan was able to win over his audience amid controversy and symbolic conflict, the Gospel Tour resulted in nearly total disaffiliation between the artist and his public.

In those Gospel shows, probably more than in any other moment in Dylan's career, we encounter the paradoxes of the interpretation of his figure. Dylan, in the common view of most baby boomers, who constituted his fan base, was the artist of the counterculture, a role he has continued to challenge since the time he jumped off the wagon of the folk revival and the early years of civil commitment and topical songwriting. Yet the "publicness" that has always characterized Dylan's figure somehow emerged counterintuitively during the years of his conversion: there he was, Dylan the reluctant prophet, suddenly speaking with full voice, delivering a message, making public statements about the dangers of war, asking his audience to follow him, preaching from a stage in a way that he had never preached, and using his music as an instrument of personal and collective transformation. The message, though, was that Jesus was coming, that his fans had to serve somebody, and that Dylan himself had to change his way of thinking.

The conversion has been one of the most discussed events in Dylan's career, but scholars and commentators have usually approached it from just two perspectives: on the one hand, they have tried to build biographical explanations as to when and why Dylan went through a phase of spiritual awakening (Williams 1980); on the other, many have focused on Dylan's works, analyzing the fractures and continuities in his songwriting and taking the conversion as a watershed that needs to be reconciled with the available visions of Dylan before and after that turning point (Gilmour 2004, 2011; Miller 2011; Webb 2006). In the process of this conceptual reconciliation, the lyrics have become autonomous from the performance, where Dylan actually communicated the conversion and made sense of it in public through his witnessing and the attempt to turn his concerts into an expression of faith, revivalism, and in some cases, altar calls, all practices typical of the vision of Evangelical Christianity that Dylan had embraced

In this chapter, thus, I will focus on the Gospel Tour and its demise in late 1980, when Dylan returned to secular songs. The problem of reception is central to understanding how Dylan and his audience competed in their definitions of the meaning of the artist, and how in this competition three major elements took center stage and created the "Born-Again Dylan." First, one should consider the intervention based on the crossing of musical genres and the definition of new criteria for the production of music that were in accord with the gospel tradition that Dylan was exploring; second, the gospel turn made sense as the social site of presentation of Dylan's different voices as singer and witness; finally, the Gospel period was served as an opportunity to produce a dialectic between the artist as a "site of memory" and the artist as the subject of action, which has characterized Dylan's career as a whole, but which was at its climax during the Gospel Tour.

Performance and the Seriousness of the Conversion

Conversions are always characterized by an extreme dynamism in a person's life. They mark in a clear way the existence of times "before" and "after"; the conversion, rather than linking the times, helps provide a justification for the attempt to follow a brand-new path that diverges greatly from the old one. Conversions, in this sense, unmake the individual and rebuild him according to a set of moral assumptions that constitute the foundations upon which the new identity is made and expressed to the public. They are, therefore, "liminal" experiences that involve the abandonment of old ways of thinking, feeling, and acting, but in which the "new" identity is still under construction; as sociologist Thomas DeGloma has argued, conversions and awakenings are characterized by the centrality of this "vocabulary of liminality" (DeGloma 2010) that is used to account for practices of distancing and recommitting, and that provides the cognitive means that allow the individual to rationalize the experience of conversion according to some repertoires and justifications that are rooted in multiple cultures, that from which a person departs and that to which he arrives following the conversion. As Rob Wilson has argued in one book dedicated to the culture of conversion in the United States (a book that also takes into consideration the personal trajectory of conversion that Dylan experienced), "conversion as such tracks a mobile trajectory between belief and prior rejection, birth, hollowing out, *and the drive to affirm rebirth*" (Wilson 2009, 88, emphasis added).

When Dylan became a convert, he offered two types of rationalization, one centered on the conversion as a sudden event, whereas the other took into consideration steps in the process of his coming to Christianity. According to Dylan, the conversion was triggered by an episode: somebody threw a silver cross onto the stage during a concert in San Diego (November 17, 1978). Quite unusually, he picked it up. Later, he claimed, he had a shocking revelation:

> There was a presence in the room that could have been anybody but Jesus.... Jesus put his hand on me.... I felt my whole body tremble.... The glory of the Lord knocked me down and picked me up. (Hilburn 1980)

By the end of the tour, Dylan was wearing the cross and had changed the lyrics of "Tangled Up in Blue," into what has become known as "the Bible version." Dylan's newfound moralizing urge deleted the mention of the "topless place": the woman was now working in "the Flamingo club." More substantial, though, was the rewriting of the fifth verse, which now carried a direct reference to the Bible instead of the book "written by an Italian poet of the 13th century." The woman Dylan meets starts quoting from the book of Jeremiah, and "every one of them words run true."[1]

This typical narrative of awakening fits well with what sociologists have often described as an episode of "passive" conversion, where a subject is converted by external, super-natural powers over which he has no control (Richardson 1985). Yet it shares important features with other narratives of transformation, "active" rather than passive; here, the sub-ject is more a seeker than a vessel, and performs his conver-sion through, and thanks to, the interaction with other people who have gone through the same experience. There are, in other words, interactional and dramaturgical elements that constitute a wider process of quest, which can be understood sociologically as a "career" (Richardson 1978). Around the mid-1970s, many in Dylan's circle had experienced a similar calling, including some of his backing musicians in Guam (the Rolling Thunder Band). Moreover, his 1978 backing group included African American women, who showed a deep religiosity, and who had been—almost invariably—raised in the Gospel tradition of African American churches and con-gregations. The fragmentary "Jesus Movement" of the late 1970s, thus, was not something that caught Dylan from the outside and by surprise, rather it came to him from within a close-knit network of colleagues and musicians.

Despite this favorable environment, however, Dylan stressed in several interviews the totally personal events of the conversion; even though he often dismissed the "born again" label, he nevertheless remarked that what happened to him was an experience of real awakening that marked a watershed in his life and inaugurated a radically new period of learning and seeking.

> Conversion takes time because you have to learn to crawl before you can walk. You have to learn to drink milk before you can eat meat. You're re-born, but like a baby. A baby doesn't know anything about this world and that's what it's like when you're re-born. You're a stranger. You have to learn all over again. God will show you what you need to know. (Hughes 1980)

This newfound feeling, which was seemingly revealed to Dylan during his intense period of study of the Bible in the first half of 1979, was to some extent hidden from the fans' view until the release of his first Christian album, *Slow Train Coming*, and the debut of a short fall tour, which kicked off with a two-week residency at the Fox Warfield theatre in San Francisco. Even the diehard fans were unsure about what to expect, as Paul Williams wrote in a short pamphlet in the immediate aftermath of the shock caused by Dylan's musical statement about his conversion:

> Something has definitely happened to Bob Dylan. This isn't the first time he's transformed himself, certainly not the first time fans have had a "new Dylan" to puzzle over. But could anyone have imagined in 1965, when Dylan fans were howling and booing that their hero had sold out by walking on stage with an electric guitar, that fourteen years later Bob Dylan would walk out on stage and sing seventeen songs every one of which makes reference to and centers around the singer's special relationship with Jesus Christ? (Williams 1980, 7)

Supposedly, they did not imagine that, and they were certainly at odds with the music, unable to come to an explanation for the sudden departure from the Dylan they had seen just a year before, touring the world with a greatest hits package. The first concert at the Warfield Theatre is telling, because it records the estrangement of an audience that, song after song, keeps waiting for the classics that never come. Dylan, in a brave but highly controversial move, marked his awakening by deciding to perform only new songs with a Christian message and scripted the show as a revivalist celebration. It was the beginning of the Gospel Tour and one of the most strained moments in his entire career.

Fox Warfield Theatre, San Francisco, November 1, 1979

The opening show came as a shock to many, but Dylan had rehearsed with a very professional band and, as usual, he had scripted the show in a very careful way. The residency at the Warfield was supposed to be a warm-up for a longer tour, but when the fracas erupted, Dylan and his management did not add new dates to the ones that were already planned. All the concerts, however, resembled the debut in San Francisco, and the format was repeated in the following legs that took Dylan into other parts of the country and Canada. On the opening night at the Warfield, Regina Havis, Helena Springs, and Mona Lisa Young delivered a passionate rendition of some Gospel classics, including a version of "This Train (Is Bound for Glory)," that had more than one link with the folk-revival Dylan had come from. The song had been sung by both Woody Guthrie and Big Bill Broonzy. Introduced by a monologue by Havis, the backing singers took the stage for roughly thirty minutes, during which they praised the saving power of the Lord, a theme that was to be central in Dylan's seventeen-song set:

1. If I've Got My Ticket, Lord
2. It's Gonna Rain
3. Look Up and Live by Faith
4. Hold My Hand, Oh Lord
5. Oh Freedom
6. This Train Is Bound for Glory

The gospel set was something totally new for the audience. The backing singers' performance was met with protests, both because of the material they were singing and because they were delaying the start of Dylan's set. Even on the first night, one can hear the audience heckling, criticism being directed both at the type and the content of songs. The two audience recordings (only one of which features the gospel set) witness a crowd that is suddenly standing against the performers. Somebody in the audience shouts, "rock and roll" midway through Havis's monologue, and calls for "Dylan!" often interrupt the songs.

After "This Train," Dylan gets on stage and opens with "Gotta Serve Somebody," "I Believe in You," and "When You Gonna Wake Up?" the three songs that were used as openers for the entire duration of the Gospel Tour. At this point, the audience was still expecting a traditional show that mixed old hits and songs from the last album, and indeed there is no sign of heckling during the first twenty minutes, as Dylan goes—quite uncomfortably—from "Gotta Serve Somebody" to the other songs that had been released on *Slow Train Coming*. The audience's reaction during the first half of the show, until a short break for the singer during which Regina Havis sang another gospel, was probably more one of anticipation of what was to come than of disappointment that the show had not featured older songs. The setlist, which Dylan changed little for the following dates, was as follows, with no room for "secular" songs:

1. Gotta Serve Somebody
2. I Believe in You
3. When You Gonna Wake Up?
4. When He Returns
5. Man Gave Names to All the Animals
6. Precious Angel
7. Slow Train
8. Covenant Woman
9. Put Your Hand in the Hand of the Man (sung by Regina Havis-McCreary)
10. Gonna Change My Way of Thinking
11. Do Right to Me Baby (Do Unto Others)
12. Solid Rock
13. Saving Grace
14. What Can I Do for You?
15. Saved
16. In the Garden

Encore:

17. Blessed Be the Name
18. Pressing On

Dylan, thus, performed his latest album—*Slow Train Coming*—in its entirety and made the brave choice to air for the first time songs that he had not even recorded in the studio, and which would become the bulk of his second gospel album, *Saved*. The first audible request for an old song came after "Man Gave Name to All the Animals," as Dylan showed no sign of being willing to play anything else than songs about his faith and his encounter with Jesus. From that moment on, things went downhill, as isolated comments from the crowd challenged a very silent Dylan. Sarcasm and direct addresses to the artist, very similar to what Dylan had witnessed in 1965–1966, followed the conclusion of any single song that Dylan sang on November 1, and he was determined to present his new stuff with hardly any interaction with the audience.

After "Gonna Change My Way of Thinking," one member of the audience can be heard shouting sarcastically, "Bobby, Jesus likes your old songs, too." Scattered members of the audience were calling for "Maggie's Farm," "Lay Lady Lay," and "Highway 61" (and in some cases even for "Is Your Love In Vain?" a minor song from the much more recent *Street-Legal*), while others were challenging explicitly Dylan's identity, with cries of, "Where's Bob Dylan?" and "We want Dylan." It was all too similar to the explicit distancing of the audience in 1965, but with the difference being that by 1979, the electric turn had been accepted, and it was the electric Dylan that the audience wanted. As Dylan rejected his previous identity on stage, the audience was reminded that it nevertheless played a major role in shaping their relationship to Dylan; issues about identity and its valence were present from the very beginning of the Gospel Tour and were exacerbated by Dylan's reluctance to talk to the audience to let them know what was going on.

Tentative as it was, if we compare it to the solid music Dylan and his band played in the following weeks, most of the times feeding themselves on the audience's anger and dissatisfaction, the debut show of the Gospel Tour featured almost all the elements that Dylan would exploit in the coming months: the renunciation of his old music, which he had probably deemed corrupt, because it was not explicitly praising his newfound Lord; the uncompromising attitude toward the audience's requests; the new sound, which owed much to the gospel tradition blended with rock music; and the clash between the message and the form, which (as we shall see) was one of the most relevant elements of contention in the performance. Yet the "new Dylan" who had seemingly emerged out of the blue at the Warfield had already released an album of Christian music, and rumors about his faith had found their way to the music press in the months before the fall tour. Why, then, was this turn so unexpected? It was received as a departure from the expectations that always exert pressure on performers to script their performances as a mix of the new and the familiar, in order to stay "true" to different representations that are held by different sectors of the audience.

During that opening night at the Warfield, challenges were coming from two directions—from Dylan to the audience with his new songs, and from the audience calling for the return of a Dylan they thought they knew well. Dylan was performing like he thought the songs could provide all the explanations that the audience needed, and the audience was taken aback by the sudden departure from their expectations. Giving so much power to the song lyrics implicitly stated that the conversion was all about the *message* that the artist was conveying. As the nights went on, and the band started filling the theater with some of the most energetic and well-played music Dylan had done in years, the message started to look insufficient, and Dylan took the stage not only with his presence and his singing, but also with his voice. The raps Dylan shared with the audience during the three legs of the Gospel Tour, with all their parables of war, Armageddon, spiritual warfare, and relief, became as important as the music, but they also revealed Dylan's own struggle with crossing genres, from intellectual rock to gospel rock, and from the rock concert as a scripted form of performance, to the evangelical celebration as a master script that had to be recognized and made sense of.

Rock or Witnessing?

"The performance was lifeless almost beyond credence." So wrote Greil Marcus (Marcus 2010, 99). "90 straight minutes of poorly played, poorly presented and often poorly written sounds" (Philip Elwood of *The San Francisco Examiner*; Elwood 1979). The *Chronicle* followed the same track: "Dylan has written some of the most banal, uninspired and inventionless songs of his career for his Jesus phase" (Selvin 1979). Dylan's God-Awful Gospel, as the notorious title of Selvin's review proclaimed sternly. The charges against Dylan were aesthetic, but they also touched the essence of a more political division that separated the path of salvation that Dylan was walking from the values and orientations of the counterculture he had contributed to shape. In years when the radical promise of rock had been watered down, and certainly played no part in the definition of any "politics," the subjugation of rock to a public statement about personal salvation seemed at best a bad career move, and at worst just one of Dylan's many betrayals.

This asymmetry was all the more manifest because the detractors of the gospel turn could exploit an image of Bob Dylan that its original creator (the artist himself) had discarded as irrelevant. Not willing to work within the boundaries of that image anymore, to the point that it suddenly became polluted in the wake of his conversion, Dylan almost gladly left it in the hands of former fans and former sympathetic critics, who built a loose, but vocal, coalition that joined the game Dylan was playing, that of drawing demarcation lines between two periods of his career and personal life. These opponents, however, changed the valence assigned to the born-again Dylan. Whereas Dylan saw himself as "saved" and could assign positive value to the new self he was projecting, the audience—or at least a good part of it, including powerful reputational entrepreneurs in the media—acted as if the new identity carried negative connotations, which revealed themselves in the poor quality of Dylan's work and in his verbatim quotations from the Bible, a sign of lack of inspiration or, worse, of successful indoctrination. In doing so, they were using the tools of rock criticism that had been shaped since the 1960s (mostly to categorize and understand Dylan's pioneering work) and that valued individuality and perceived originality as important markers of authenticity. What was happening was, for want of a better term, a *subcultural clash* between visions that had been proposed in the 1960s in opposition to mainstream American culture and that valued their outsiderness as a means to keep members in a state of perceived purity, whether it was the aesthetic purity defined through the contrast between the artistic merits of rock and the slick ingenuity of "pop," or the more demanding purity that was defined in religious terms by the Evangelical subculture to which Dylan had committed himself. This culture itself struggled to create its own boundaries and aesthetics of music, in the conflict between "separational" and "integrational" visions, according to which singers should primarily be perceived as Christians witnessing their faith, or as singers who were most of all entertainers and *also* Christians (see especially Howard and Streck 1999, 49–110).

What critics seem to have missed in this game of boundaries, though, was Dylan's willing submission to a system that was not only a system of beliefs, but also and not secondarily a system of practices, which conditioned his performances and brought them across the divide that separated rock music from the emerging aesthetic domain of Contemporary Christian Music, which had been provisionally fixed in the previous decade in the context of the widespread and lively subcultural milieu of the "Jesus Movement." Critics focused so much on words and content that they overlooked almost without exception the liturgical implications of Dylan's conversion and how he attempted to translate them on stage by exploiting a "prophetic" narrative. It was an ambivalent account, because the "prophetic" tone had previously been a powerful representational feature in the definition of the secular Dylan, and Dylan thus struggled between two contradictory statements: the old Dylan was not "saved," and therefore his words had to be questioned as inauthentic vis-à-vis the new word he was spreading, yet even that old image, which had been praised as "prophetic" by his supporters, could be understood as a starting point of the process that came to maturation in his embrace of Christianity.

At some point during the Gospel Tour, when the songs became insufficient to convey the message of salvation he was trying to make public, Dylan tried to reconcile these two identities, by seizing the representations that had been built around him in the early 1960s and translating the political prophecy to the new contents of a religious one:

> I told you "The Times They Are A-Changing," and they did! I said the answer was "Blowin' in the Wind," and it was! And I'm saying to you now, Jesus is coming back, and he is! There is no other way to salvation. (Albuquerque, December 5, 1979)[2]

However, the assumption of a prophetic role inaugurated a tension with the audience that made the problem of the recognition of Dylan the "prophet" even bigger, as Dylan himself acknowledged on stage in Omaha (January 25, 1980) during the second Gospel Tour:

> Years ago they used . . . , said I was a prophet. I used to say, "No I'm not a prophet." They say, "Yes you are, you're a prophet. I said, "No it's not me." They used to say, "You sure are a prophet." They used to convince me I was a prophet. Now I

come out and say Jesus Christ is the answer. They say, "Bob Dylan's no prophet." They just can't handle it.

The religious revival into which Dylan immersed himself had a dominantly prophetic tone—the millenarian vision of a world that would soon face the ultimate Judgment, coupled with an emerging social and religious movement that took the witnessing of the possibility of salvation as a central discursive element. "We're living in the end of times," was a common remark that Dylan made almost from the beginning of the tour. And in perilous times, he seemed to argue, one had to hang on to the solid rock that Jesus Christ represented for him and other Jesus people of the 1970s. Indeed, the song that was centered on this message, "Solid Rock," proved to be one of the strongest that Dylan has ever played in his career, full of conviction and zeal that were missing from the version Dylan recorded for his second Christian album, *Saved,* in 1980.

"Solid Rock" is a song that establishes a direct connection between Jesus as the son of God and the singer, because it was for him that Jesus was "chastised," "hated," and "rejected." The only available choice for the believer is to recognize that he "won't let go and [he] can't let go no more." The public witnessing of the conversion, as a sign that one had been saved and had thus established a personal, almost direct relationship with God and especially with the figure of Jesus Christ, played a major role. It coupled a militant vision of evangelization with the idea that the saved was outside society and at the same time active within it, a theme that has been present in Christian thought at least since the evangelizing zeal of Saint Paul.

In this context, the practice of witnessing became even more important than the system of ideas that was at the center of the evangelical vision. The Jesus movement had surely an ideology; it was a lively subculture that resembled a "cultural front" that opposed mainstream American society as the counterculture had opposed it (and many saved Christians came from that very milieu, as did some preachers and many musicians of the first wave of Contemporary Christian Music); but most of all it was a culture of practice, where the reality of salvation had to be performed and made public in order to fulfill the idea that the personal acceptance of salvation had to be complemented by the effort to reach out to those who were outside, "too blind to see" as Dylan sang in "Precious Angel." We find this attitude in many street preachers, like Lonnie Frisbee, who engaged in a dialogue from inside the counterculture, and also among the first wave of born-again musicians like Keith Green and Larry Norman. All these figures shared not only a system of beliefs, but most of all the practices of expression of religious faith (including the use of music, the public witnessing, and the altar calls) that crossed from the church to the stage and back.

Dylan's Gospel Tour, with its rejection of secular material and the raps between songs, was thus embedded in this culture of witnessing that others (including Dylan's old acquaintance Johnny Cash) had embraced and performed since the early 1970s. The prophetic tone and the prophetic mask that Dylan wore made sense within this context, where the public expression of faith played a role in the remaking of the individual and also provided an example for those who were not yet saved. To some extent, witnessing (and this is what Dylan was doing in his effort to make his faith public) requires the audience to be a co-participant: it is active testimony that involves the audience in a dialogue that is aimed at their conversion, and not simply as an expression of faith that the audience records in a passive way. In doing so, Dylan was playing (maybe not intentionally) with the criterion of participation that regulated the activism of the audience within the frame of the rock concert. He was, in other words, working outside the rules that constituted rock music as a genre, contaminating them with the rules that regulated the public expression of faith in the evangelical religious revival, and with other rules, much closer to the musical tradition he has always explored, which were at the core of the black gospel tradition.

Gospel Rock and the Politics of Genre

The issue of genre stands at the center of the production and the interpretation of art works (Holt 2007). Generic labels—writes Simon Frith—work both "as a way of organizing the playing process" and "as a way of organizing the listening process" (Frith 1996, 87–88). Adapting the work of Franco

Fabbri (1982), Frith argues that genre is governed by rules that are socially accepted both by the performers and by the audience. They configure a space of agreement, a shared culture about music, the work of music and its performance, and provide a set of standards for the execution and the interpretation of a performance (be it a performance on record or in concert). Interpretive conflict can, however, result from genre work in specific moments of communication and interaction between the artist and the audience, which sometimes can produce the performance of the unexpected, the sudden recombination of musical meanings and cultural categories, and the creation of crossover sounds and new meanings (Brackett 2002).

In Dylan's gospel concerts we see genre work as the explicit reconfiguration of styles and themes and as the abandonment of *some* of the categories through which he had previously been interpreted. What was Dylan doing? Was it a rock concert or a religious call, and were these "songs," or "prayers" and "sermons"? This tension revealed itself not simply in a battle of definitions, but first and foremost in a battle for genre attribution, where style and content functioned as parameters for the categorization of Dylan's work. The entire shows were interspersed with gospel songs, and the structure of the concerts was organized in such a way as to give the strong impression of a religious celebration in a newer key that imported elements from the rock counterculture. The intrusion of gospel was very effective at the performative level, and the opening set by one of the female singers revealed that Dylan had given a lot of attention to the narrative organization of the show. However, it was during the gospel songs that the calls for rock and roll tended to disturb the singer and question her legitimacy to be on the stage in the setting of what should have been a secular celebration. Certainly, this intrusion was perceived as external to the format of the concerts and not as one of its defining elements. It was less an introduction to Dylan than an active element that helped define the tone and goals of the show, especially if we consider that Dylan did not limit the more traditional gospel songs to the beginning, where they could have served a self-contained function, but used a gospel track—sung by one of the singers—as the performance that marked the transition from his first set to the second, where he played mostly new songs that dealt less with the discovery of faith than with the ineluctability of Judgment. Traditional gospel numbers were thus used to punctuate Dylan's performance and also to set the genre to which the concert could be ascribed and the way the audience should have shaped their expectations.

The mix of gospel and rock characterized the tours of 1979 and 1980; Dylan, in this context, was doing something more daring and at the same time more advanced, if we compare it with other Contemporary Christian Music acts of the period. These singers were, more or less, working within genres, like Johnny Cash, or trying to make rock legitimate for the Evangelical audience. Dylan was crossing genres, mixing the rock tradition to which he seemed to have belonged and just another aspect of the black American tradition he has always explored and exploited with the respect of a loving thief. Instead of referring to the blues and the electric rhythm and blues of the 1950s, he was now drawing key elements from a much older gospel and spiritual tradition. This inspiration was explicit in the lyrics, in some of the arrangements, and in the scripts that regulated the shows.

As a music genre, gospel does not simply codify the content and the style of performance, and it does not rest only on a stereotypical description of the performer in terms of racial identity and religious commitment. It articulates in a peculiar way the dialectic between the individual and the collective in the process of making music together. The "audience" in gospel is a fluid collectivity rather than a fixed entity. In some respect, gospel music aims at a transformation of the audience into a co-performer, and traces of this attenuation of the actor–audience boundaries are often incorporated in the dynamics of call-and-response between the lead and the backing singers, and between them on stage and the audience. Performance in gospel, as in many other instances of traditional music (even in the case of invented traditions or traditionalized modern forms), rests on the values and cultural codes of a "participatory performance," as opposed to a "presentational" one (Turino 2008). Participatory performance is an "artistic practice in which there are no artist-audience distinctions, only participants and potential participants performing different roles, and the primary goal is to involve the maximum number of people in some performance role" (Turino 2008, 28). This interaction between the performer and the audience is crucial for its performative success. It involves playing together and a coordination in vivo that makes the boundaries between the stage and the audience less fixed, as well as other participatory practices that "fuse" actor and audience, like clapping and singing along, which are of course of crucial importance in the performance of gospel.

These goals are often achieved by lyrical simplicity and the definition of times when the audience can intervene and construct the song in the performance together with the lead singer. Gospel lyrics are characterized by repetitiveness, syntactic simplicity, and intertextuality, in their reference to passages of the Bible that the audience of believers can recognize, all for the sake of performance and the creation of communion between the performer and the audience, and for the transformation of the "audience" into a co-performer. The simple structure of Dylan's songs in this period clashes with the complexity of his 1960s work, but hints to the way he was adhering to the rules of a genre that valued highly the simplicity of the message and the possibility of remembering the lyrics through repetition. Lyrics in the gospel song, indeed, are often constructed so that they can produce a participatory reaction in the audience: they carry the seeds for audience participation, something that Dylan's backing singers tried to achieve when they encouraged the audience to clap or sing along. In order to achieve this goal, however, the text must be simple and the performance able to convey immediately the meaning of the words and reduce the room for interpretation and ambiguity.

The construction of Dylan as an intellectual singer-songwriter, and also as a songwriter *for* an intellectual public, had made words central to his work and music a secondary aspect. The Gospel Tour offered a different view of the relationship between message and music, as a consequence of the change of frame and genre. Yet the message of Dylan's music was probably as important here as it had been in the past, once understood through the constraints within which he was working and presenting his music: the culture of witnessing that was central in the vision of Evangelical Christianity that he had embraced; the rules of competence and performance that constituted the gospel tradition by which he had been influenced; and, finally, the definition of genres and the way they defined two different visions of Dylan, the Dylan of the past and the Dylan of the present. The poor reception of the first Gospel concerts, which meant also that Dylan had not met his performative goals, made genre work even more explicit, as Dylan exploited more and more the theatrical tools that came from within the Christian tradition and assumed the role of a witnessing preacher, rather than letting the songs give all the testimony.

Singing and Preaching on Stage: The Problem of Dylan's Speaking Voice

Spoken word was present from the very beginning in the Gospel Tour, though it was confined to the opening gospel set. Dylan was initially silent, true to his principle that "the songs speak for themselves." Besides a brief comment that "God don't make promises he can't keep," it took Dylan until November 4 to start speaking—and not just singing—about his new faith. Again, it was during the introduction to "Solid Rock" that the spoken word entered the concerts, initially with a very short remark:

> Thank you. Alright, we all know we're living in the end of the end of times. So you'll need something strong to hang on to. This song is called "Hanging On to a Solid Rock Made Before the End of the World."

By the time the residency at the Warfield was coming to its conclusion, Dylan had considerably extended his raps to the audience; he was offering more articulated arguments, which were usually placed in strategic points of the concert: in the introduction to "Slow Train Coming," right before the gospel number in the middle of Dylan's show, and in the usual spot before "Solid Rock." The remark about the end of times, now with a more explicit reference to the situation in Iran, was moved before "Slow Train," and became longer:

> You know we read in the newspaper every day, what a horrible situation this world is in. Now God chooses to do these things in this world to confound the wise. Anyway, we know

this world is going to be destroyed. We know that. Christ will set up his kingdom in Jerusalem for a thousand years, where the lion will lie down with the lamb. Have you heard that before? [Applause] Have you heard that before? [Applause] I'm just curious to know, how many believe that? [More Applause] Alright. This is called "Slow Train Coming." It's been coming a long time, and it's picking up speed. (San Francisco, November 16, 1979)

This apocalyptic vision, possibly influenced by Hal Lindsey's evangelical best-seller *The Late Great Planet Earth* (Lindsey 1970), accompanied Dylan in all his raps during the Gospel Tour, until May 1980. In all these cases, what Dylan tried to achieve (sometimes succeeding, sometimes failing) was a momentary affiliation of the audience with his words, through the use of a series of rhetorical questions, itself a technique of dramatization that is imported from participatory religious rituals, where the audience is required to be involved and confirm the vision of the preacher. The questions *produce* a connection between the singer and the audience, an involvement, however transitory, in the performance, and the impression that there is a situational bond between two otherwise very different roles. These rhetorical questions attenuated in part the asymmetry between the performer and the audience in a double direction: they were supposed to work as a sign of agreement or affiliation on the audience's part, but also as a sign that Dylan had momentarily crossed the line that separated him from the public, involving the public in the performance.

As a recent convert, Dylan was preaching enthusiastically both with his songs and with his raps. Dylan's confidence in talking to the audience was a central part of the performance of the conversion on stage. As the sermons grew longer, Dylan used the voice in two ways, to extend the meaning of the performance beyond the formulaic character of the gospel songs he was performing, and to shape his stage persona in the intermediate stage between artist and preacher. These uses of the voice were, again, embedded in the performative prescriptions of witnessing, but often they were confronted and questioned by the audience's different attitudes toward the practice of witnessing. Dylan played for quite diverse audiences during the first leg of the Gospel Tour, from the believers that crowded the venue in Santa Monica, to a much more angry audience in Tempe, Arizona. Preaching to the converted (as the title of a bootleg goes) usually made Dylan more talkative, and the originally short remark that "God don't make promises that he can't keep," heard for the first time in San Francisco, was further articulated:

> I don't know what kind of god you believe in, but I believe in a god that can raise the dead. He does it all the time, every day. Now there's certain men, you know, many of them who live right in this town who seek to lead you astray. You be careful now. The real God, the real God, the one and only God, he don't make promises that he don't keep. That's how you can tell he's the real God.

In some cases, the same comment was more confrontational, and it revealed Dylan's feeling for and awareness of the type of audience he was playing for, like in Albuquerque:

> Alright. Thank you. I don't know what god you believe in. I believe in a god that can raise the dead. Unless your god can do that, he ain't no god. (December 5, 1979)

As the tour approached its conclusion, indeed, the confrontation with the audience became more explicit, and the attacks on Dylan's status as a performer more verbally violent. Tempe and Tucson were the venues where this disaffiliation between Dylan and the audience took its most extreme form, and certainly the intensity of the heckling, yells, and degradation of Dylan's role as a performer in Tempe was as great as it was in the most controversial moments in 1965 and 1966. On November 26, 1979, there were at least twenty episodes of audible disaffiliation, countered by very little applause, aimed at shutting up the hecklers. The tension increased during a long monologue that Dylan recited as the introduction to "When You Gonna Wake Up?" The moments when Dylan spoke, rather than the ones when he sang, were the main opportunities for his opponents to voice their disapproval, which makes Dylan's raps central to the understanding of his religious enthusiasm and the shape it took on stage.

Some examples taken from that monologue reveal that the breach between Dylan and the audience was a battle for the definition of the artist and a total rejection of his message to the audience:

> DYLAN: What a rude bunch tonight, huh? You all know how to be real rude. You know about the spirit of the anti-Christ? Does anybody here know about that? So anyway, this certain guru, you wanna hear about this guru? So anyhow,
>
> AUDIENCE: Rock and Roll! Shut up!
>
> DYLAN: Alright, so this guru, he made a film of himself. He had one of these big conventions. He does have a convention I think every so often like once a month, he'll go to a big city.
>
> YELLS FROM THE AUDIENCE: Praise the Lord with Puke! Shut that guy up! Rock and Roll!
>
> DYLAN: You still want to rock 'n' roll? I'll tell you what the two kinds of people are. Don't matter how much money you got, there's only two kinds of people: there are saved people, and there's lost people.

The calls for rock and roll were a recurrent element of the audience's interaction with Dylan, together with the requests for his old songs. For fans, the traits of this older and recognized Dylan were totally disconnected from the current performance, and Dylan's desire to use his symbolic power to operate a transformation in the audience and to witness his own conversion was met with rejection. This battle to fix the meaning of the artist involved, in other words, the meaning of Dylan for his public and a set of expectations about the way he had to be and carry himself, which were simultaneously shattered and reconfigured in the performance. Artistic reputation relies on a set of assumptions that the performing artist will be consistent with the established image and will not challenge the expectations that the audience has of him. Yet, Dylan had always been praised for his ability and his willingness to discard expectations in his quest for innovation in music, be that the innovation in songwriting that characterized his folk years or the innovation of genre that made the electric turn meaningful.

Because Dylan was doing both things on stage (being true to his shape-shifting image and defying expectations in the local setting of the performance), he was in a sense confirming the core ideas on which his reputation was grounded. Yet, at the same time, he was contesting equally important assumptions about the role of the artist and artistry in rock music.

First, he was questioning the audience's claim about the intimacy they shared with the artist and the overall dynamics between distance and proximity upon which celebrity is constructed. There is always some sense in which members of the audience "know" the artist, and this feeling of familiarity shapes individual relations with the artist in a world characterized by fandom and the attenuation of the boundaries between the artist and the fan. By presenting himself on stage as a preacher, and by attempting to involve the audience in the dogmas of his newly found faith, Dylan challenged this feeling of sameness, complicity, and common cause that in many situations is a requisite of the audience's involvement with the artist. Second, with the decision to perform only religious material, and to acquire a didactic tone in his speeches, Dylan created a tension between seriousness and leisure in the concerts. Rock has always depicted itself as a "serious" genre, as opposed to pop, in this, retaining at least some of the assumptions typical of its folk roots. The seriousness of genre rests on an autonomous vision of rock as work that—in its best instances—can aspire to "high" art, and certainly the perception of Dylan as a poet and an intellectual artist has contributed to shape his reputation. The seriousness of the genre, however, is often constructed with reference to rock's proximity to secular poetry; religious proselytizing of the type that Dylan performed in his speeches, on the contrary, is based on the seriousness of an explicit connection to the sacred.

Leisure and seriousness stood, thus, as two fundamental and non-reconcilable alternatives, with Dylan challenging the audience into a confrontation about the meaning of the shows, as serious and sacred, as opposed to the different articulation of seriousness and entertainment that the audience held. Sometimes, the audience made a point for leisure by quoting one of Dylan's most well-known lines:

AUDIENCE MEMBER: Everybody must get stoned!
DYLAN: I'll tell you about getting stoned. What do you want to know about getting stoned?

This very short exchange leads to the final, third point of rearticulation of the basic assumptions about the identity of the performer in a rock concert that Dylan challenged in the Gospel Tour. In his speeches, as well as in his songs, Dylan dismissed and reaffirmed his "secular" identity as a performer, as a rock musician, while simultaneously trying to reinstate his legitimacy as an artist *in* the rock tradition even in the moment of personal transition. "Rock and roll" was something that the audience requested countless times during the concerts, mixing with some confusion the genre and the theme of music. In Tucson, Dylan rebutted to a quite exasperated audience:

AUDIENCE: Rock 'n' roll!

DYLAN: Rock 'n' roll ... (indecipherable) I knew how to rock 'n' roll when you was in diapers. You know about the end of times though? I'm just curious. I know you know about rock 'n' roll, but do you know about the end of times? The last day?

Thus, while the audience was questioning Dylan's right to do what he was doing on stage, but never his competence on rock matters, Dylan moved the confrontation from music to a different area, where he could question the audience's competence on the religious matters that for him deserved to be at the center of the performance. However, these were perceived by the audience as standing outside the frame of the rock concert, and Dylan's attempt to bring them in the frame revealed a breach of the informal contract that is signed between audiences and performers, that they both recognize their competence to act and perform in such a way to meet expectations. In the context of the conversion, this mutual recognition stood outside the scripts that Dylan was following, and the effort to have his vision acknowledged conflicted with the audience's ideas about the way he should perform. The private events of the conversion could not affect—they thought—the artist's presentation in public, whereas, for Dylan, the conversion was total, and it had to be dealt with in a totalizing way that produced a new image, which had to be extended—amid negative reactions —to the audience. It was in this process that the visions held by the artist and the audience became separated from each other, and the communion was shattered, producing an opposition that made Dylan—as a convert who had been saved and had acquired a new knowledge and a new awareness—separate from his audience, as this fragment of conversation reveals:

AUDIENCE MEMBER: Bullshit!

DYLAN: "Bullshit?" [loud heckling] Some of those people out there don't like the Lord? Don't know the Lord? What is it? Don't you like the Lord, or don't you know the Lord? Which one of those is it? [loud heckling; someone shouts: "I don't care!"] You don't care? Don't care?? I know you don't care. I didn't use to. (January 14, 1980, before "Gonna Change My Way of Thinking")

"I didn't use to" is a telltale remark. The Gospel Tour, unlike many other instances when Dylan has been almost silent on stage, featured this intrusion of personal testimony in a very ambivalent way, as evidence of Dylan's willingness to witness his faith, and as an attempt to justify (in a self-confident way) his choice and get in control of the audience both by preaching and by directly addressing members of the audience. The problem of performing "Bob Dylan" in the Gospel Tour (and partially in the tour that followed it, when Dylan started to play his old songs again) lies in the web of contradictions that governs the public expression of transitions. The voice that Dylan used in the tour, when he sang and most of all when he spoke to the audience, worked as the means of expression of the new identity of the artist, and as a comment to the songs, in the attempt to offer a public rationalization of the conversion. Dylan's voice, as well as his music, is so important to understanding the conversion and the meanings that the artist associated with it, including his role as an artist and the public dimension of his conversion.

This battle for identity was crucial in the performance of the last point that I am taking into consideration in this chapter. The dialectic between the artist as a symbol embedded in culture (Dylan's broader reputation as recognized by his fans and even the larger public), highly resistant to transformation, and the artist as the subject of action.

Dylan as Performer and Symbol
in the Gospel Tour

During the three legs of the Gospel Tour, Dylan walked a very narrow path, because he was trying to connect himself to his established image as a musician while making the conversion a permanent turning point in his career, the focalizing event that marked a separation between the past and the present. The old Dylan became nevertheless a major point of reference for all those who wanted to contest the nature of the performance and its core symbolic assumptions. The appropriation of a specific image of Dylan by the audience characterized the confrontation that emerged in the Gospel Tour, which Dylan tried to reduce when it became clear that he could not advance his new image without making room for the emergence of a powerful counter-discourse about reputation and the artist as a symbol.

The first tour in which Dylan started playing his old songs after the vehement musical radicalism of the Gospel Tour was an important occasion for witnessing the dialectic between the preconstructed images of the artist, and Dylan's attempt to reach a balance, performative as well as representational, between the image of the "Bob Dylan" that emerged from the conversion and the ones that were pressuring him from the past. The tour, billed as "A Musical Retrospective" by promoter Bill Graham, was marketed as a show where Dylan was going to include in the setlist old songs "that had a special significance to him" and that were consistent with his new faith. The comeback of the old songs had been anticipated by a radio ad in the days preceding the debut, where Dylan could be heard rehearsing new arrangements of his old hits. There was thus anticipation, but also a belief that the script of the show was going to be different from that of the previous year.

However, the first concert of the fall 1980 tour (again at the Warfield, the place where things began and where they changed after a stormy year) still resembled in many ways the typical Gospel concert of 1979–1980. The changes were initially minimal: The first two songs had been the standard openers since November 1979, the warning that everybody "Gotta Serve Somebody," and Dylan's personal statement of faith in "I Believe in You." The third song, quite unexpectedly, was "Like a Rolling Stone," followed by a gospel number sung by Carolyn Dennis. "How does it feel?" sang Dylan, "to be without a home, with no direction home, like a complete unknown," words that reached a deeper meaning in the context of the musical retrospective tour, and Dylan was not to change the position of "Like a Rolling Stone" in the setlist for most of the tour. This first performance, after more than two years in which no "familiar" or "old" song was played, was striking. "Like a Rolling Stone" is Dylan's manifesto; at the Warfield, it started in a quite unrecognizable way as—for three or four seconds—the band tried to get into it. As soon as the audience realized that the first old song of the night was being performed, there was an eruption of cheers from those who recognized the iconic chord sequence. Then, as soon as Dylan finally sang the first line ("Once upon a time," Dylan telling a story while busy struggling with the collision of the old and the new) he gets his audience back, for the six minutes it takes him to run through the song.

The opening night was probably closer to what Dylan saw as his "Musical Retrospective," a show very similar—probably too much, if we trust the negative reviews that appeared in the press—to those he had offered during the Gospel Tour. Dylan played seventeen songs, but only six of them (including a cover of Dion's "Abraham, Martin, and John") were songs from his secular period: the aforementioned "Like a Rolling Stone," "Girl of the North Country," "Just Like a Woman," "Señor," and "Blowing in the Wind." Only the latter two can be identified as songs that allow a religious reading; the other three seem to explore either characters who are lost on the wrong side of the tracks ("Like a Rolling Stone" and "Just Like a Woman") or, quite interestingly, distance and lost love, a metaphor to indicate somebody that the conversion has separated from the artist.

The reconnection with the past was, thus, largely incomplete during the first concerts. However, as the tour proceeded, Dylan started playing more songs (the standard setlist, by the end of the tour, would feature twenty-four songs) and including a more diverse selection from his older catalogue. By the time he played the last concert of the tour (in Portland, December 4, 1980), the gospel songs were barely eleven out of twenty-five. The tour was, thus, characterized by the progressive reappropriation of his old material, and by the presentation on stage of a performance that could meet the favor of the audience. Which begs the question, how can an artist who has disowned the work that is at the origin of his fame *convincingly* step back and claim the authority to be associated with it again? Although the motivations behind this choice may well have been instrumental (a decline in record and ticket sales, the will to keep a fan base), the decision to include old songs in the show, and the parallel marginalization, as the tour progressed, of the more recent gospel material, was both an act of communication and an attempt to reshape the image of the artist. Performance, in this sense, was the site for the reconstruction of the image of the artist, and an arena for recognition, which involved both Dylan's presentation and the audience's sanction, with both pragmatic and more extended representational consequences.

Was the reintroduction of old songs deemed sufficient by all actors involved to seal the breach inaugurated by Dylan's departure from his past? In some respect, the nineteen concerts of the fall 1980 tour were crucial in closing a musically fundamentalist phase in Dylan's career. However, a close look at the setlists and at the recordings allows a more accurate understanding of the representational consequences of the conversion on Dylan's role as a performer, as well as a consideration of his attempts to rationalize in concert what looked like a surrender to the audience (which, to some extent, it was, if we consider the way the show changed from the first concerts to the later ones). The structure of the show remained very similar to the radically inventive gospel shows of 1979 and early 1980. Each of them opened with the backing singers on stage, although the introductory monologue was gone, and gospel numbers marked the transition between one set and another. The Musical Retrospective Tour, thus, retained some memory of the Gospel Tour in the scripts of performance, although the deep themes of witnessing that had characterized it barely came to the surface. The performance was organized in such a way that the old Dylan was presented on stage, creating in the meantime a friction between two images of the artist. However, although during the three legs of the Gospel Tour this tension was rooted in the declaration that the past could not pollute the present, the Musical Retrospective was the expression of the attempt to reconcile in the same setting these two visions of Bob Dylan.

At least in the first shows, Dylan was staying true to the philosophy of the Gospel Tour, the old songs being at best an intrusion in what he perceived as the "authentic" performance he was willing to offer. Out of fifteen songs that he played at almost every concert (eighteen or nineteen times), only five were old songs, suggesting that the meat of the show was made of gospel songs, very recent and thematically homogeneous. Moreover, there was much more variability among the old songs compared with the newer material (roughly half of the songs he played were from his three latest albums, *Slow Train Coming, Saved,* and the forthcoming *Shot of Love*). This original script changed toward the end of the tour, when old songs began to appear more and more, to the point that they accounted for more than 60 percent of the songs played at every concert.

A second interesting point regarded the way Dylan intervened on his public presentation, not only by performing his old songs but also by reconnecting his stage persona to established representations that were available to his public. In the Musical Retrospective Tour, acoustic arrangements and the use of the harmonica came back after they had been neglected during the previous tour. Notably, all the acoustic songs were from the pre-Christian period. Because the image of Dylan with an acoustic guitar has always been powerful among the audience, when he performed solo on stage, or with the very bare accompaniment of electric piano and autoharp, he was able to present on stage a vision of Dylan more attuned to the stereotype held by many attendees.

The third aspect dealt with Dylan's positioning in the field of rock music, a claim about legitimacy, which he achieved both by performing his songs and by being joined on stage by selected guests who were associated with his reputation as a rock artist and performer. Michael Bloomfield (who had played guitar at Newport and at the "Like a Rolling Stone" session) made his last public appearance before his untimely death due to a heroin overdose. Maria Muldaur (whom Dylan knew from the early days in the folk scene) and bluegrass mandolin player David Grisman joined Dylan on stage. Jerry Garcia and Carlos Santana offered the embodiment of "rock," while Roger McGuinn jumped in for "Mr. Tambourine Man" and "Knocking on Heaven's Door." These guests provided evidence of Dylan's integration into the realm of rock, and of his right to play with his identity as both a rock artist and a religious performer (Muldaur and McGuinn were themselves recent converts). Playing music with those stars offered Dylan the opportunity to reclaim his public image as a rock artist, which had been questioned by the audience and rejected by the artist himself during the Gospel Tour.

Finally, Dylan tried to reconnect himself with the mythic narratives of rock and tradition. Dylan was usually very talkative, but the tone and content of his raps were radically different from the God-inspired sermons that had created the breach with the audience during the Gospel Tour. Quite interestingly, Dylan chose to talk almost exclusively when introducing his old songs or the covers. After a few days, and possibly as an oblique answer to the negative reviews that were published in the San Francisco press, he included in the set an old folk standard, "Mary from the Wild Moor," and used it as a rebuttal to the critics:

> People are always asking me about old songs and new songs. Anyway, this is a real old song. I used to sing this before I even wrote any songs. One of them old Southern Mountain ballads, I guess everybody used to do them. Last time we played, I think it was in Tucson, . . . there was a review in the newspapers that I'd like to get straight. The man that came to the show and reviewed it didn't know where all the songs came from. Anyway this one here he said was about Jesus being born in the manger. Well that's not entirely true about this song. It's just an old Southern Mountain ballad, that's all it is, about somebody dyin' in the snowstorm. Anyway, it's called "Mary and the Wild Moor." (San Diego, November 26, 1980)

The performance, with Dylan on acoustic guitar and Regina Havis on autoharp (an instrument that connotes the tradition and the southern country of the Carter Family), was a high point until the end of the tour. Nor was it the only occasion when Dylan commented on tradition, and—via tradition—on his authenticity. Dylan's storytelling went into tradition, and in this way he explored (and made available to the audience) the idea that tradition itself, the folk tradition but also the more recent and malleable tradition of rock, was always characterized by the simultaneous presence of permanence and change. Consider the following excerpt, taken from the recording of the November 12, 1980, show:

> This is a twelve-string guitar. First time I heard a twelve-string guitar was played by Leadbelly, don't know if you've heard of him? Anyway, he was a prisoner in, I guess it was Texas State Prison, and I forget what his real name was, but people just called him Leadbelly. [Shout from the audience: "Huddie Leadbetter!"] He was recorded by a man named Alan Lomax, I don't know if you've heard of him? Great man, he's done a lot of good for music.

This sort of name-dropping reached two objectives: First, Dylan showed on stage his competence in secular music, reminding the audience that he had the authority to compare himself to other artists, and that the path he was walking had been walked by many others, with whom he felt a deep connection (Leadbelly, as one of the godfathers of the folk revival, holds a special significance because he embodied one of Dylan's roots as an artist); second, Dylan tried to communicate to the audience the idea that change was essential to popular music, and indeed the tale about Leadbelly continued in this direction:

> At first he was just doing prison songs and stuff like that. Same man that recorded him also recorded Muddy Waters before Muddy Waters became a big name. Anyway, Leadbelly did most of those kind of songs. He'd been out of prison for some time when he decided to do children's songs and people said oh, why did Leadbelly change? Some people liked the old ones, some people liked the new ones. Some people liked both songs. But he didn't change, he was the same man!

The ex-convict and the mythic rock star shared, in this view, a common identity trait, their ability to change while staying true to their own authenticity. When Dylan played Seattle, he treated local hero Jimi Hendrix (a musician in the pantheon of rock, like Leadbelly was in the pantheon of folk) in a very similar way:

> We been here before in Seattle. I always like to come to the home of Jimi Hendrix. I met Jimi Hendrix in New York when

he was there [more calls from the audience]. All right, all right! Oh, thank you! Anyway we're gonna do a song now. I wish Jimi was around now, 'cause I know he'd record it ["Slow Train Coming" follows].

These four aspects of the presentation of the actor in the performance (definition of the script, intervention on his identity, connection with the past, and use of legitimizing figures) helped Dylan redefine his role as an artist and prove his authority to speak from within the field of secular music. This re-appropriation of his role took place in a context characterized by questions about Dylan's detachment as a performer from his older self, but also from the values he represented and that had settled in a set of representations that guided the audience's reception of the performance. What was at stake, thus, was the contemporary character of Dylan as an object of representation, as well as the much deeper and more troublesome claim about how an artist can advance a claim about authenticity when he departs from the culture that has helped him construct his authenticity.

Conclusions

Dylan failed to project the meaning of the conversion in the Gospel Tour, because the high authority he had for the audience did not translate automatically into the acceptance of the new discourse about his right to produce works of art that were inconsistent with his past. To some extent, even the most revolutionary artist is condemned to repeat his work, and here lies a puzzle of artistic creation, the fact that the *conservation* of the aesthetic forms and meanings can be interpreted as revolutionary art. The disaffiliation with the audience took place within this dilemma of presentation and had lasting effects on Dylan's career. Audience disaffiliation, in the Gospel Tour, resulted from the friction between available symbolic resources that he had created and represented him as a *progressive performer* (the term carries almost no political connotation) and the difficulty to interpret his performance according to that progressive framework. The conversion was performed on stage because its communication played a great part in the religious culture that Dylan had accepted as his own, but in doing so Dylan created a space for contestation, which had to be reduced by an equally public expression of "redress," which happened when he went back to his older songs.

Therefore, both Dylan's departure from and return to his consolidated image have to be assessed from within the boundaries of performance, and performance must be considered as a fundamental setting for the debate about Dylan's authenticity during the Gospel Tour. By the late 1970s, Dylan's authenticity—which had been shaped originally according to the rules of the folk revival, therefore, in the context of a restricted field—had become fixed and not questioned regardless of artistic achievement and the ups and downs of his career: His achievements could be panned (as happened to *Self Portrait, Renaldo and Clara,* and Tour 1978), but the background of authenticity was hardly questioned, and it provided symbolic resources for the definition of the "real Dylan." With the Gospel Tour and the public, dramatized expression of the conversion, Dylan touched for the first time the core elements of his authenticity, and rejected them. In doing so, however, he left them open to the audience's appropriation, inaugurating a conflict in which he could claim to be "authentic" (and especially an authentic convert and a true believer), but could not exploit to his advantage the authentic narrative that had been built around him. In other words, the memory of "Bob Dylan"—now free floating and ready to be used as a weapon by the audience —provided a powerful counterimage that the artist could not use effectively without stepping back into the game of authenticity that he had discarded as "inauthentic."

As I will show in the next chapter, this tension between the past and the present has become a permanent trait through which Dylan has been defined, and especially since the 1980s, when Dylan's figure started to become more and more canonic and memorialized. However, the outcome of these latter efforts has been different, and its analysis requires a much deeper investigation of collective memory in popular music, especially the tension between the different memory projects that have characterized Dylan and his audiences and that have paradoxically resulted not in interpretive conflict but in what today seems a permanent affiliation of the audience to Dylan and in a parallel attempt on Dylan's side to produce his own discourse on a wider memory of American tradition from the perceived periphery of "Bob Dylan" as an icon.

Notes

1. The new version of "Tangled Up in Blue" that was played at the end of 1978 carried reference to different passages of the Scriptures. In the beginning, as Williams (1994, 134) has noted, Dylan was referring to the Gospel according to Matthew, but the "chapter 33" Dylan mentioned does not exist. Later, he changed the lyrics to refer to the book of Jeremiah.

2. Dylan's addresses to the audience and his religious raps have been transcribed from the available recordings of the shows. I have them checked and modified when necessary, with two existing fan projects documenting the Gospel Tour. Watt Alexander's "The Gospel Project" is an annotated guide to the first Gospel Tour of November–December 1979 (www.angelfire.com/rant/gospelproject/, accessed online May 3, 2011). Olof Björner has documented every single concert and setlist of Dylan's career, including stage talk, a fact that is absolutely valuable when it comes to researching Dylan's conversion and practices of witnessing on stage. Björner's files can be accessed at www.bjorner .com/bob.htm. Accessed online April 8, 2012.

◇

FIVE

Back Where I Come From

Bob Dylan's Memory Projects
and the Never Ending Tour

On February 11, 2010, Bob Dylan appeared before President Barack Obama for a musical celebration of the civil rights era. It was a puzzling performance for several reasons, not least Dylan's now ragged and growly voice, which sounds so different from what fans and casual listeners have sculpted in their memories. It was, nonetheless, a notable performance, with Dylan making a rare appearance with an acoustic guitar (one so beat up, it might have been with him since the 1960s) to sing a very subdued version of "The Times They Are A-Changin'," an anthem that turned, for four minutes, into an admission of weariness and a disturbing lullaby. A few months earlier, Dylan had made another, quite similar, appearance on a PBS show celebrating Peoples' Songs and the American folk tradition. This time, backed by electric guitar and piano, he sang (in a sweet tone that suits what's left of his voice) one of Woody Guthrie's dust bowl ballads, "Do-Re-Mi." When juxtaposed, the two songs make for a startling comparison. Dylan not only owns the sixties and their popular culture because they were partially created through his work and influence on other musicians; he also is master of a counterculture that has deeper roots, the vision of American folk music, which was shaped and channeled through the waves of the folk revival from the 1930s through

131

the 1960s, when Dylan acted as both the recognized herald of the revival and its executioner.

Both performances mark a peculiar social space, where the memory of the past presses into the current work of the artist and functions as an unavoidable reference. This has been the paradox of Dylan's reputation over the past twenty years, one that touches deep aspects of the relationship between artists, public representations, and broader collective memories. As much as he has become an iconic figure, encapsulated unwillingly in a nostalgic look at the 1960s, Dylan's work seems also to point to a different realm of memory, the long and deep tradition of American musical heritage, of which Dylan has appointed himself the social organizer, the entrepreneur, the bard, and the manager. In an interview given to *Rolling Stone* just a few months after the release of *"Love and Theft"* (itself a record haunted by musical memories that build a complex intertextual web), Dylan acknowledged the core of this project: "Every one of the records I have made has emanated from the entire panorama of what America is to me. America, to me, is a rising tide that lifts all ships, and I've never really sought inspiration from other types of music" (Gilmore 2001b).

The paradox between Dylan as an object of memory and Dylan as a subject of memory-making is created in the interaction with this background. Dylan's America has become more and more an explicit reference, not in political but in musical and cultural terms, as Dylan has grown older and all his projects have tried to capture a vision of tradition that has been filtered in a distinctive Dylan-esque way. In turn, this consideration of the past—made of "love and theft," direct appropriations and more subtle transformations—has contributed greatly to Dylan's renaissance as an artist over the past fifteen years, a period in which he has explored the endless streams of America's heritage, old folk songs and urban rhythm and blues, vaudeville and Christmas carols, forgotten artists who survive only in the dusty grooves of recordings made during the Great Depression and modern songwriters who seemingly share with Dylan the same vision of authenticity.[1] These multifaceted influences have found their way into all the projects that Dylan has used to convey his vision of authenticity to the public: folk albums (*Good As I Been to You* and *World Gone Wrong*, at the beginning of the

1990s, when he seemed to have lost track and "his groove": Yaffe 2011), a "greatest hits albums without the hits" like *"Love and Theft,"* plus a handful of covers recorded for tributes to Johnny Cash, Woody Guthrie, Hank Williams, Ralph Stanley, and Doc Pomus; a radio show like *Theme Time Radio Hour,* which has presented everything from Memphis Minnie and The Clash, lifting its format from an old, forgotten show that Alan Lomax ran in the 1940s (*Back Where I Come From,* hence the title of this chapter); movies and documentaries; an autobiography; finally, touring, which seems to be where all these multimedia projects really come from.

Dylan's artistic and musical renaissance has indeed taken place in the eddy of what Stephen Scobie has characterized as the "years of performance" (Scobie 2003, 24–26), which have found their locus in the metaphor of the Never Ending Tour (hereafter, NET), Dylan's project of playing roughly one hundred gigs a year since 1988. For more than two decades, and more than 2,000 concerts, Dylan has built one of the biggest examples of the relationship between an artist and the stage, and particularly between Dylan's work and his performance on the stage, where stellar performances can be followed by abysmal ones, greatest hits by one-off performances, a tour where Dylan presents, endlessly, new personae and new approaches to his music (Muir 2001). The NET, from this point of view, is less a tour in traditional terms than a traveling show, Dylan's own attempt to move his work concretely beyond time and the burden of his image, the embodiment and fulfillment of the original idea of the circus that he explored in the mid-1970s, as something that goes on forever and that creates a performative space for creativity and the transformation of songs. It is my contention that the NET offered Dylan the opportunity to fire back at the attempts to categorize him as only the object of nostalgia and a one-sided memorialized icon and produce his own, highly idiosyncratic narrative about the American landscape. The NET has been (and still is, at least in part) Dylan's preferred social site for the definition of authenticity. And it is surprising that while the public is busy creating "Bob Dylan" as a memorialized object, Dylan himself is involved, through the NET and thanks to the opportunities that the NET has created, in a parallel process of memory work that involves performance as a means to create multiple facets of memory: the memory of Dylan (with all the constraints posed by the representations of the artist that circulate in multiple arenas), the memory of American popular music and vernacular tradition, and the definition of a notion of authenticity that links the past and the present, which is surprisingly close, though radically different on crucial points, to the one Dylan first abandoned in the 1960s when he bade good-bye to his fellow travelers in the folk revival.

Images of Dylan and the Representational Challenge of the NET

A personal memoir: In June 2011 I was waiting in line to see Bob Dylan play in Milan. I had no ticket, and I had made the trip there, hoping some fan had a spare (luckily, I was able to get one at the last minute, and I was rewarded with a performance of "Visions of Johanna," my all-time favorite of Dylan's songs). My first Dylan concert had been almost exactly twenty years before, and among the crowd waiting in line there were people I had seen many, many times over the years, people who attend multiple shows in several countries and follow entire tours. Then, there were those who could be considered die-hard fans outside the NET experience, who had seen Dylan in concert five or six times. Finally, teenagers who were as young as I was when I attended my first concert, who were there for the first time, understandably excited. It was a diverse crowd, and indeed the experience of seeing Bob Dylan live—whether as an opportunity to see a "legend" or as something that has become so frequent it is part of your routine—meant many different things to all of them.

Seeing Dylan in concert has become both an affordable and a common opportunity, at least if one lives in Europe or in the United States. The mystery of previous decades has been replaced by availability, an inflation of appearances (still around 100 a year) that makes Dylan visible for his fans. Yet, this is a kind of visibility that seldom interacts with the discourses that are constructed around Dylan, with the reproduction of Dylan's image in musical and cultural circles, and with many representations that powerfully construct our vision of Bob Dylan. Despite Dylan's visibility as a performing artist, the NET has provided him the opportunity to "disappear" from public view, because his tour does not generate the buzz and the expectations typical of those of other stars. At the same time, he is creating a new set of standards for the reception of his music that are largely constructed within and are dependent on the NET. Narratives and stories, as "shorthand ways" to think about Bob Dylan (Fine 2001, 7) continue to circulate, often through the reproduction of images that have gained authority and that still focus on the powerful representations of Dylan as an artist who embodies the spirit of the 1960s. Yet, performances (especially the kind of centrality of performance that the NET ensures) constitute a relatively safe space (safe, because it is not subject to continuous media scrutiny) for artistic reinvention and presentation. The NET, in some sense, is not an "event" that attracts media coverage or large crowds, and in this context Dylan can be freed of many pressures, not least those dealing with the necessity to present "Bob Dylan" in such a way as to create a sort of iconic proximity between the artist as he works on stage and the symbol that has been sculpted in memory.

The detachment of these two aspects of Dylan's figure at times is almost complete, but it would make little sense without a consideration of Dylan's attitude toward the stage, and to his songs as they are transformed, reconstructed, and deconstructed in the NET. In many cases, the NET has been useful to Dylan's purpose, the deflagration of his myth, through a series of not necessarily successful repeated performances. Indeed, the NET has been an uneven effort, where the good and the bad have been equally presented in performance, and where Dylan has—for long periods—constructed his shows upon what seemed like "unprofessionalism," improvisation, and sometimes even a lack of care for the audiences he was entertaining.

A NET show can be disappointing, when it is experienced as a projection in performance of the range of meanings that constitute Bob Dylan's image and as a performance that must align with the standards that mandate the presentation of a rock star, who is faithful to his image, establishes a relationship with his audience, and includes the "show elements" of performance that the audience has come to rely on. The NET offers none of these; on the contrary, the performance is built and organized around a series of distances that mark a difference between the established, available images of Bob Dylan and the way he sounds, sings, and presents his work.

There are indeed multiple projects that contribute to the definition of Bob Dylan's image, and they rely in different ways on selected areas of Dylan's career trajectory. Some—like the ongoing project of the *Bootleg Series* or Martin Scorsese's documentary *No Direction Home*[2]—exploit the iconicity of Dylan's 1960s image, while at the same time making it relatively autonomous from that of Dylan's later career. In a certain sense, Dylan's semiretirement in 1966 helped detach the early part of his career and make it autonomous from the rest of his career trajectory. Those early images constitute the hard core of what his work represents to a wider public. And, over several decades, those images have built a series of expectations about how "Bob Dylan" has to *be* as an artist and where he stands in the field of popular music. I have illustrated these conflicts in previous chapters, and I have shown to what extent those representations have been effective. Every transition Dylan made in order to live up to his image as a protean artist was counterinterpreted, with, for example, the poet being contrasted with the topical singer, the rock artist with the poet, the gospel preacher and saved Christian with the rock artist, and so on.

To some extent, these images speak to Dylan's exceptionality, according to which the reasons for his greatness can be found only in Dylan himself. Dylan, indeed, has often only been compared to himself, to what he accomplished in the past, and to the roles he has played throughout his career. Dylan appears to acknowledge the representational power of all these personae in the short introduction that precedes his entrance on stage, which is usually read by one of the roadies:

> Good evening Ladies and Gentlemen! Please welcome the poet laureate of rock 'n' roll. The voice of the promise of the '60s counterculture. The guy who forced folk into bed with rock, who donned makeup in the '70s and disappeared into a haze of substance abuse, who emerged to "find Jesus," who was written off as a has-been by the end of the '80s, and who suddenly shifted gears and released some of the strongest music of his career beginning in the mid-'90s. Ladies and gentlemen, Columbia recording artist, Bob Dylan.

Since 2002, this pastiche of roles and masks that Dylan has taken on over the course of his career has greeted concert audiences, reminding them of the turning points in Dylan's trajectory and of the new critical acclaim that has brought him back to a more centralized position in terms of achievements, praise, and influence. This condensed biography highlights changes, high and low points, and ultimately the fact that Bob Dylan's career has been more complex and less straightforward than the celebratory narrative that is constructed around him would suggest. As a result, external representations of "Bob Dylan" and his status in the broader domain of popular culture come to the concerts and present historical references to the artist even before the songs are sung. These references are also embedded in the performance and serve to attenuate the boundaries (emotional, cognitive, and practical) between the past and the present. Indeed, Dylan can play a song from any of those career phases, although songs can be disguised as something "other" than the original, faithful to Dylan's idea that the performances released on record often serve only as blueprints for the songs as performed in public.

Performances work on these boundaries, presenting the artist and allowing room for the comparison of images that are created by activities outside performance (such as interviews, record releases, reproduction of iconic elements, biographies) and those that are experienced in the moment the artist performs (how the audience receives the artist). All of these activities interact, contributing to the generation of stable (if not necessarily shared) images of the artist. When it comes to circulated media, performances can be an intrusion, especially when the way an artist presents himself in the performance does not align with existing media representations. Dylan's voice, for example, has lost its nasal tone, it's been years since he played an acoustic guitar during the NET, and his last solo performance with acoustic and harmonica dates back to 1993. Aging, and aesthetic choices, have produced a different notion of Dylan as a performer, which is in stark contrast to the image of Dylan that is held by a large part of his public.

The old Dylan, however, is always present as a reference that cannot be avoided. These representations that are produced through various types of media contribute to the fixation of the artist's image and to the distribution of information among audiences. This is not a one-way flow, from the producers to the receivers, but rather a cooperative (and competitive) collective work that involves producers, members of the media (like critics, writers, and nowadays bloggers), and audiences, which are exposed to various cultural products and, in turn, make some critical use of them. In Dylan's case, these activities have been instrumental in producing a two-sided image of "Bob Dylan," both as the poet laureate of rock and roll, fixed in a cliché that has existed since the 1960s and that effectively makes use of Dylan's body of work from that decade, and a more contemporary view of Dylan, as a modern songwriter who, in his later years, has been able to position himself as the social organizer of a wider tradition of American music, to which he claims to legitimately belong.

The interaction between these two images creates a peculiar space for performance. Because Dylan seems to have found a new dimension as a performing artist, seeing his work on stage more and more as a "trade" than an "event" to be celebrated as the periodic tour of a rock star of his status, his reputation (which is formed by those condensed images) seems to constitute the context within which his performances (erratic, shambolic, terrific, moving, depending on the year, the tour, the night, the song, or even the line he sings in a particular moment) must be interpreted. Hence, the long-lived tension between what Dylan was or was not on stage and what Dylan was expected to be as an artist and as a performer.

Two parallel discourses have contributed to Dylan's image in the NET. One was the relatively autonomous and mediated discourse that was aimed at the reproduction of Dylan's iconic status. The other took place almost exclusively in the NET, defining a new canon and new standards for the interpretation of Dylan as a performing artist. These two discourses stand as poles around which the conversation about Bob Dylan (artist of the past, artist in the present) and the contexts that he embodies are produced. The border between these two discursive configurations that contribute to the artist's image is not impermeable. Many times, Dylan has been pressured to perform his past. At Woodstock 1994, a celebration of the original "three days of peace and music," he was introduced on stage in a way that brought the past immediately to the audience's attention: "You waited twenty-five years," hinting to the fact that Dylan did not play at the original Woodstock Festival in 1969. In 1992, a very uncomfortable Dylan mumbled through "It's Alright Ma" and "Song to Woody," during a special spot in the celebration of the thirty years since his debut. Therefore, images of Bob Dylan are often used and circulated to confront the more behind-the-scenes project that goes on in the NET, that of reinvention and reconnection between the artist, his song-book, and his audience.

For a man who claimed that he was Bob Dylan "only when he had to be," and was himself the rest of the time, these consolidated features were often harmful, and it is worth noting that the entire NET project was originally designed as a means to escape these pressures. Dylan has often been perceived as "inauthentic" when he has given the audience what they were craving (like in 1974, 1978, 1984, and 1986–1987). On the contrary, some of his most effective moments on stage were those that defined a new subjectivity and centrality of the singer (like during the Rolling Thunder Revue) or those that were very controversial (like in 1966 and during the Gospel Tour) and fueled by problematic interactions with his audience. In other words, trying to align his performances to the public image of "Bob Dylan" has often meant a detachment from the vision of authenticity that constitutes a great part of what Dylan stands for as an artist. What is ironic is that the NET, too, has often been dismissed as the presentation of an inauthentic Dylan, or a Dylan who is totally disconnected from his work: Dylan chews his songs and renders them a mere pretext for transformation; he doesn't engage his audience in those activities that construct a sense of proximity (true to the assumption that the songs need to be central in the context of a performance); he seems to be singing "badly" while, for an individual who has been exposed to the experience of the NET and the peculiarities of Dylan's phrasing, he is engaged in doing something—constructing his song on stage—that is seen as an unrepeatable experience, which has to be witnessed in the here and now of the performance. Although this assumption about Dylan's inauthenticity might be true for certain periods, when Dylan was not interested in performing music (and in some cases too intoxicated to even remember the words of songs he had sung for decades), the logic of presentation and performance as embraced in the NET served to affirm Dylan's authenticity, especially the authenticity of his performance.

The disenchantment I have mentioned seems to have been what Dylan tried to get away from when he embarked on the NET, and Dylan's constructed distance from his audience (to the extent that he does not speak on stage, except when he introduces the band) seems to be a totally different strategy for projecting his role as a performing artist to the public and to ensure the centrality of songs instead of the centrality of the icon who sings on stage. In *Chronicles*, he has remarked that "the public had been fed a steady diet of my complete recordings on disc for years, but my live performances never seemed to capture the inner spirit of the songs. . . . The intimacy, among other things, was gone" (Dylan 2004b, 145–146). Gone in shows that looked too similar, packed with the same songs and unsophisticated vocal performances, Dylan too shy to break new ground by revisiting his old songs. With all its metaphors (a new singing technique, a revelation experienced in a jazz bar that may or may not have happened) what Dylan writes in *Chronicles* about this dark period of his career seems open and sincere, that he had lost the connection with his audience and that he was "just above a club act" (Dylan 2004b, 155), both in terms of sales and rewards, and very close to walking down nostalgia lane to disappear in a series of small gigs. Indeed, he confessed to radio interviewer Martin Bronstein that he had almost called it quits, in a move that resembled his decision to get out of the music business in 1965, in the weeks before writing that "long piece of vomit," "Like a Rolling Stone."[3] What happened, then, that created a new connection between Dylan and his songs, and what role did performances play, as the dominant arena where the new meanings of Bob Dylan have been formed and prepared for the public—those of a Dylan who is able to stand on his feet as a timeless cultural icon who has bracketed the importance of his role in the 1960s and is able, as historian Sean Wilentz argues, to play "tricks with the past and present, memory and history," and who is able to "reclaim the present by reclaiming the past" (Wilentz 2010, 263–264)?

Dylan, Dialogue, and Memory

A first answer can be found in Dylan's own words. In later years, Dylan has repeatedly challenged the myth of originality, calling for a renewed vision of his authenticity that pays homage, in lyrics, arrangements, and performance, to a pantheon of American music that walks alongside him, even though oftentimes this is a march of the dead: Woody Guthrie walks with Charley Patton, Robert Johnson with Hank Williams, Buddy Holly with the Carter Family. It is a network of cultural references that is distinctly American: it goes beyond the established image of Dylan as the "poet" of contemporary popular music and also beyond his association with rock music. As *Theme Time Radio Hour* and Dylan's last albums since *"Love and Theft"* clearly demonstrate, Dylan's roots predate rock, and this connection to older singers and song forms (acoustic blues, Tin Pan Alley popular songs, minstrelsy) represent a fundamental part of Dylan's approach to the collective memory of American popular music and—via these memorialized artifacts—to the memory of "Bob Dylan" himself. He has acknowledged repeatedly, denying the romantic originality of his songs and their dependence on roots that he has explored in several periods of his career: "My songs, what makes them different is that there's a foundation to them. That's why they are still around.... [My songs] are standing on a strong foundation, and subliminally that's what people are hearing. Those old songs are my lexicon and my prayer book" (Pareles 1997). Dylan's problem, for much of the 1980s and for years since the beginning of the NET, was to treat his own songs, and not only the traditions he has explored and appropriated, as a lexicon, conveying the impression that he inhabits them as much as he inhabits a timeless realm of American roots music.

These two processes, of cultural reference to the past and of re-creation of Dylan's authenticity through the performance of his songs, have characterized the whole trajectory of the NET from its very first nights. In June 1988, Dylan surprisingly revisited (after more than twenty-five years) songs that he had originally recorded for his debut album in 1962. The first night of the NET in Concord (June 7, 1988) featured "Man of Constant Sorrow," and the second show saw "Baby Let Me Follow You Down" back for a one-off performance in the acoustic set. It was the song that Dylan had used to shock his audience during his tour with The Hawks in 1966, and for once, it was back to the world of folk from which Dylan had kidnapped it, back where Memphis Minnie, Blind Boy Fuller, and the Reverend Gary Davis (all singers of "original" versions of the song) belonged: it had gone from acoustic to electric, and back. Starting in 1988, another song from *Bob Dylan* entered this process of reconstruction, although its NET incarnation endured more lastingly. It was "Pretty Peggy-O," a hidden gem from Dylan's catalogue, whose precious character can be witnessed only by immersing oneself in the dialogic philosophy of the NET. "Pretty Peggy-O" is an Americanized version of the Scottish ballad "The Bonnie Lass of Fyvie," which became a very popular song during the folk revival (with Joan Baez and Simon and Garfunkel, among others, recording their own versions). Dylan's original version is joyful, almost a parody of the revivalist attitude, sung so fast as to convey the impression that the protagonist of the song wants to get a quick answer and avoid Peggy having second thoughts. Dylan's NET arrangement bears little resemblance to the song he recorded. Rather, it is a faithful cover of the Grateful Dead's version, which, in turn, reworks the melody of Joan Baez's arrangement. It is slower, much slower, and Dylan's adult, aging voice makes the song simultaneously a plea for love and a menace when he sings "your cities I will burn."

The Never Ending Tour is constructed upon these appropriations. On good nights (like in Binghamton 1992, or Albany 1997), "Pretty Peggy-O" reaches the ethereal level, where Dylan's voice and Bucky Baxter's pedal steel guitar are able to take it. Yet, sometimes unbeknownst to the audience, the performance constructs a web of references, that brings to the surface and to experience not only the artist's engagement with the song, but also the possibility of multiple readings that contribute to the perception of Dylan's artistic versatility. And Dylan seems to be at his most versatile when he ventures outside his songs and plays a game of individual authenticity and appropriation that is centered around his performance of covers (Solis 2010). Covers, during the NET in particular, are essential to this process through which Dylan entertains a relationship with other artists and other images of the American landscape, whether the song in question is "Hallelujah" played in Canada as homage to Leonard Cohen, or "Heartbreak Hotel," sung on the anniversary of Elvis Presley's death. In some sense, these songs are part of what Robert Polito has called Bob Dylan's "memory palace" (Polito 2009), where different traditions are filtered through the interpretation of the artist and used as pretext for the presentation of an alternative Dylan, who is not just a self-centered artist with his own repertoire and his own—huge—image, but who is also an interpreter who embodies an alternative tradition in performance, which only occasionally finds its way onto the albums.

There is, indeed, another side of the coin. If the Dylan we witness through the NET reaches out to other works in order to communicate them to his audience, it is also true that most memory work (and to some extent the most problematic) is carried out in the interpretation of his own songs. Here, the image of "Bob Dylan" that audiences have before them constrains the interpretation of the performance; it functions like a capsule that includes, and holds together, the artist and his work. The Never Ending Tour started with an implicit assertion of what for Dylan had become a problem that was affecting his career and trapping him in a troubled relationship with his past. How could he treat his own songs—and not only the "memory palace" he has admitted to loving—as a lexicon, a corpus that is in itself memorialized and that serves important functions in the evaluation of the artist?

The first song ever performed in the Never Ending Tour was also Dylan's first live performance of "Subterranean Homesick Blues" (Concord, June 7, 1988). It was hardly an unplanned choice, especially because it became the standard opener for the tour, and it was performed seventy-one times (the most performed song in 1988). "Subterranean Homesick Blues" holds a peculiar position in the Dylan canon, because it summarizes the transitions that Dylan underwent when he abandoned folk and embraced electricity. Not only does it have a special status as the iconic soundtrack of the opening scene of his documentary *Dont Look Back*, it was also

Dylan's first single to break into the top 40, and one that signified his attempt to build a new persona while stepping out of the folk revival. He even remarked in an interview for the *Les Crane Show* that he was the author of "Subterranean Homesick Blues," rather than of "Blowin' in the Wind." It is also important for more subtle reasons: it pays homage to early rock and roll, with its intertextual and melodic reminiscences of Chuck Berry's "Too Much Monkey Business," and it has deep roots in a song that Pete Seeger and Woody Guthrie wrote, "Taking it Easy"; moreover, it contains some of the most individualistic lyrics by Dylan, including the memorable lines "you don't need a weatherman / to know which way the wind blows," and "don't follow leaders / watch those parking meters."

"Subterranean Homesick Blues," thus, goes back to the days of Dylan's maximum influence on popular music, yet in a non-nostalgic way, as the artist plays with the unfamiliar and the unexpected (two adjectives that fit the NET well). It helps carry into the concert musical connotations that have to do with genre—"this is rock and roll!"—and with the reputation of the artist as an innovator. It also signals Dylan's attempt to achieve a rebirth through performed music that was in his mind when he assembled the tour and scripted its format.

Both "Pretty Peggy-O" and "Subterranean Homesick Blues" (along with many other songs that have been performed during the NET, not necessarily the most successful in performative terms or songs that belong to the Dylan canon as "classics") are elements of Dylan's attempt to redefine his authenticity in the late 1980s and early 1990s in two ways: the reevaluation of his own repertoire, achieved through the exploration of almost his entire catalogue; and the reevaluation of traditions, as a means to claim individual and artistic authenticity. Dylan's authenticity in the NET, though, has always been a fabricated, and highly inclusive, vision of tradition, that ranged from Johnny Cash ("Give My Love to Rose" and "Folsom Prison Blues") to Stephen Foster ("Hard Times"), from the Stanley Brothers to Buddy Holly. At the beginning of the Never Ending Tour, this engagement with tradition carried multiple meanings. Not only was Dylan seemingly more willing to incorporate a rich musical past into his concerts, he was doing it in such a way as to articulate a double discourse. First, the concerts were occasions for the artist to confront his own past, and second, they served to portray Dylan as a performer in a wider landscape of popular and vernacular music. Those two purposes overlapped, yet they had some distinctive elements. In a sense, Dylan was challenging the claim about the autonomy of the artist made by the wider culture that had created him, acknowledging both the debt he owed to some roots that were constitutive of his music and whose origins were in the oral culture (a culture where the individual artist is more the performer than the sole creator of the verse), and the debt he owed to his contemporaries (Dylan's homages to other authors acquired special significance in this context).

This de-individualization of the artist as a social symbol is a fundamental assumption of the social production of belonging to a tradition. It is, borrowing the words of Russian literary critic and cultural historian Mikhail Bakhtin, a "re-accentuation" of the Other (Bakhtin 1981), cultural forms and products that are scattered across the spectrum of time that are not identified unequivocally with Dylan, but to which Dylan—all the discourses about his individuality notwithstanding—seems to belong almost "naturally." This feeling of natural belonging, which is on the contrary as socially constructed as any other claim about an artist's image, is the outcome of Dylan's practices of authenticity. However, the NET seems to entertain a peculiar relationship with authenticity, because it can never obliterate the stream of practices and discourses that create "Bob Dylan" as a symbol. Two Dylans, as subject and object of collective memory, are always in a state of constant tension, and on many occasions one of these discourses has been dominant at the expense of the other.

Unplugged and the Supper Club: Two Ways of Performing "Bob Dylan"

This conundrum can be clearly revealed in the description of two shows—and their related efforts to produce specific images of Bob Dylan—that participate in different ways in the logic of the NET: Dylan's participation in MTV's series *Unplugged* and Dylan's attempt (in 1993 at the Supper Club in

New York) to produce his own unplugged album, in line with the performative authenticity and the memory projects that have been central in the NET. To date, *Unplugged* is one of the most striking examples of how expectations about Dylan (and the image of Dylan as an artist of the 1960s who can be subjugated to a nostalgic vision) can harm a performance. *Unplugged* was not unsuccessful in commercial terms (almost hitting the top 20 in the United States), but from the video, the official record, and the bootleg recordings of the two shows that Dylan played to assemble the complete televised product, one can see an expressive fracture between Dylan's act in the 1990s, his attempts to reshape his approach to music and his songs, and the vision of Dylan as a symbol that gave form to *Unplugged*.

Allegedly, Dylan wanted to perform a show with many traditional folk songs, but was advised to do otherwise by his label and the producers of MTV:

> I wasn't quite sure how to do it and what material to use. I would have liked to do old folk songs with acoustic instruments, but there was a lot of input from other sources as to what would be right for the MTV audience. The record company said, "You can't do that, it's too obscure." At one time, I would have argued, but there's no point. OK, so what's not obscure? They said "Knockin' on Heaven's Door." (Gundersen 1995, 12D)

Dylan's performance for *Unplugged* was characterized by many elements of nostalgia and seemed almost an enactment of "Dylan" in many of its stereotypical features. He wore a polka-dot shirt and Ray-Ban sunglasses, reminiscent of his appearance at Newport in 1965. Nor was the outfit the only nostalgic element that characterized the *Unplugged* performance. Usually, Dylan's backing band on the NET used a pedal steel guitar to recreate the parts that in many records were played by the organ or the piano (until 2002, when Dylan started playing the electric piano and the organ himself). For *Unplugged*, and only for *Unplugged*, an organ player was added, to produce a sound more similar to Dylan's old records, the trilogy of the "thin wild mercury sound."

The widely viewed *Unplugged*, thus, reproduced an already available vision of Dylan, very close to the core narrative that constituted his reputation among a wide audience: Dylan was identified mostly with the 1960s, and they were represented in the performance of songs like "With God on Our Side" and "The Times They Are A-Changin'." Dylan's presentation of himself as a performer relied on aesthetic and thematic elements that were not part of the standard act he was showcasing in the NET at that time, and sound elements that were thought to be characteristic of Dylan's 1960s work, like that of the Hammond organ, were heavily present. As an atypical performance, *Unplugged* fed the process of memorialization of Dylan in a subtle way. It presented Bob Dylan as he should sound in the 1990s, but also as a performer who had gone through a slow evolution from the 1960s, from which he had retained important stylistic elements. In this sense, *Unplugged* exploited the extra-performative representation of Dylan in an attempt to meet the demands of an audience that was familiar with what Dylan used to represent and not his most recent self-image. The artist as a performer stands out as the figure that embodies an other-directed reputation.

However, in the same years when *Unplugged* seemingly aimed at the reproduction of Dylan as a symbol, Dylan himself was making efforts in the direction of a more articulated project of memorialization. Rather than merely reenacting his figure in concert and on record, he was shaping the NET and his sparse studio work in ways intended to make a claim about his embodiment of a wider American tradition, especially with the reconnection to folk music and traditionalized sounds. These efforts eventually resulted in his acoustic records *Good As I Been to You* and *World Gone Wrong* and in the still unavailable "Bromberg Sessions," a project that involved Dylan diving into the tradition epitomized by Harry Smith's *Anthology,* and which unfortunately was shelved.[4]

Unknown to many but his fans, Dylan tried to produce his own unplugged show a year before he ultimately surrendered to MTV. Dylan played four shows at the Supper Club in New York (November 16 and 17, 1993) and intended to release a video or live record with his current band. The Supper Club shows are very different from *Unplugged,* and comparing them to the released record is helpful in pointing out the differences between the portrayal of authenticity that Dylan performs within the logic of the NET and the more extemporaneous attempts that result from external pressures and demands. At the Supper Club, Dylan played nineteen songs, only two of which were songs that he was later to play during the shooting of the *Unplugged* show ("I Want You" and "Absolutely Sweet Marie," neither of which made it to the final record), and six of which were traditionals. No complete video has been officially released or has been leaked to the fan community, but the shows are available as bootleg recordings. These recordings reveal much about the way Dylan conceived his own all-acoustic concert, which was much more in line with the narratives he tried to bring to his performances in the NET shows. The folk tradition features heavily in the shows, either with songs that Dylan had recorded or released in his acoustic albums of the early 1990s, or with the one-off performance of Blind Boy Fuller's "Weeping Willow."

The entire trajectory of Dylan's career was represented in the shows, with songs from the folk period (only "My Back Pages"), his mid-1960s trilogy (three songs), his post-incident period (three songs), the 1970s (two songs), the 1980s (three songs), and the covers. The Supper Club, thus, was a retrospective of Dylan's career much more than *Unplugged* was; with the obscurities and the traditional songs, these shows fit well into the image that Dylan had tried to present on stage during the NET and were, on the other hand, at odds with the vision of the artist that *Unplugged* tried to convey.

Even though *Unplugged* and the Supper Club both centered on the artist, their representational outcome could not have been more different, in terms of adding or subtracting to Dylan's image as filtered through live experience (or through the media experience of sound and video). The Supper Club shows try to accentuate Dylan's special symbolic character, by positioning the artist against a cultural background that he brings to the surface as an entrepreneur of tradition, pointing explicitly to a set of cultural references (American folk songs, the lack of hits except for "Lay Lady Lay") that have been constructed in years through the live experience of the Never Ending Tour. In this regard, they show the two logics that have characterized the NET since the beginning: the logic of appropriation that Dylan has mastered since his first adventures in the folk revival, and the logic of transformation of Dylan's own songs. An example of this transformation can clearly be seen in Dylan's Supper Club rendition of "My Back Pages," a song that entered the NET as a transformed cultural artifact, performed first as an electric, guitar-driven cover of The Byrds' 1967 version (Cincinnati, Ohio, June 22, 1988) and later as a slow acoustic number, where the fiddle plays the perfect counterpart to Dylan's weary voice. Both attempts work—and seem to work—only from the symbolic periphery of what we interpret as "Bob Dylan," away from the canonized figure that still exerts its seductive power on audiences and that encapsulates Dylan into a set of representational assumptions that have been reproduced from the 1960s. As I will argue, many images of "Bob Dylan" point toward this selective memorialization, to which performance plays an ancillary role. The NET, on the contrary, seems to counter the effects of these practices by fundamentally altering the rules of the memory game in which Dylan and his multiple audiences are involved.

World Gone Wrong: A Sound for Timeless Times

The NET is not a single project, and Dylan himself dismissed the label as early as 1993 in the sleeve notes he wrote for his folk album *World Gone Wrong,* when he warned the audience not to "be bewildered by the Never Ending Tour chatter. There was a Never Ending Tour but it ended in 1991." Much more recently (Brinkley 2009), he seems to have disowned completely a label, which, rightly or wrongly, has come to characterize Dylan's experience in concert for the past two decades:

> Critics should know there is no such thing as forever. Does anybody call Henry Ford a Never Ending Car Builder? Anybody ever say that Duke Ellington was on a Never Ending Bandstand Tour? These days, people are lucky to have a job. Any job. So critics might be uncomfortable with my working so much. Anybody with a trade can work as long as they want. A carpenter, an electrician. They don't necessarily need to retire. (Brinkley 2009, 44)

Rather, the NET is a succession of tours that might sound very different in terms of approach, songs, arrangements, and performative success. But there are also common traits that can link a concert in Allentown, Pennsylvania (July 12, 1989), to one in Spokane, Washington (October 5, 2001), to an appearance before 250,000 people in Saugerties, New York, in August 1994, and to a show at the United Palace Theatre in New York in November 2009. Dylan's repertoire is just one of those traits, and even in this case, the changes to which it has been subjected in particular years or occasions— changes that can only happen in the NET and be available to those who surrender to the experiences that the NET creates —contribute to the creation of the live experience of "Bob Dylan" as something peculiar and partially disconnected from the memories that hold an iconic vision of Bob Dylan. Lee Marshall (2007, 189–197) argues convincingly that the NET moves the reception of Dylan's work beyond the "recording consciousness" that constructs a set of expectations about the way the artist should sound and about how he should be remembered, toward a more direct experience of the song as a performance that is centered on what happens here and now. The NET takes this logic of change to an extreme, where the original version functions at best as a sketched canvas, and the version as played in concert achieves a unique status. Sometimes these changes are macroscopic, and "Shelter from the Storm" (to give just one example of the songs whose structure allows broad transformations) can become a radically different song altogether, where the "original" as recorded for *Blood on the Tracks* becomes a distant reference point, diluted by the scripts that Dylan constructs for his performance and by the arrangements that guide the performance of the song. As Dylan explained in an interview with Murray Englehart:

> The arrangement is the architecture of the song. And that's why our performances are so effective these days, because measure for measure we don't stray from the actual structure of the song. And once the architecture is in place, a song can be done in an endless amount of ways. (1999, reprinted in Cott 2006, 407)

The tension between the permanence of the structure and the changes that affect the songs the moment Dylan sings them is what Dylan pursues through his performances, as a means to achieve a "diminution of the NET audience's recording consciousness" (Marshall 2007, 210–211). The different arrangements of "Shelter from the Storm" in 1988–1994, summer 1994, 1995, and the one-off arrangement that Dylan played in Japan in 1997, all refer dialogically to the original version, but they take the song from a periphery that can emerge only in performance, in the effort to distance the song from its reference as fixed in the record. Here, what marks the difference is Dylan's singing and phrasing. Dylan's voice is itself an instrument of performative power, which avoids duplication and delivers a song, even a line, or just a few words, calling attention to unexpected passages or vocal solutions that testify to Dylan's richness as a performer. It is his voice that makes two performances of the same song, like "Visions of Johanna," fascinating in their subtle departure from both the canon and the listeners' previous experiences. A clear example of this can be heard in the way Dylan sings "the harmonica plays, the skeleton keys and the rain" in Chicago 2001, or "the ghost of electricity howls in the bones of her face" in Münster 2000. These ephemeral experiences, which would be condemned to oblivion if it weren't for bootleggers, form much of the NET's game of distances and differences: they cannot be found anywhere else in Dylan's work, and they have to be witnessed as Dylan performs them, or searched in a game of collecting and training one's ear to the nuances of Dylan's performances, which takes the listener deeper into the NET experience. Among commentators, Paul Williams has been the most vocal supporter of the exceptionality of the NET as a domain of experience guided by and constructed through Dylan's performances and idiosyncratic approach to the delivery of his songs. For Williams, a work like "Visions of Johanna," as played in New York in 1999, comes to life as a phoenix from her ashes, "not a repeat of a work of art created back in 1966. It is unmistakably a great work of art created at the time of its performance. Something new and original and thrilling" (Williams 2004b, xi). Williams probably goes too far in stressing the emergent qualities of the experience of the song, because a song is always part of a network that includes previous performances that build it as a peculiar object of memory (whether these are the performance as it appears on the record or other performances that have constructed it in concert), but certainly this impression and this perceived originality come from the distance that Dylan tries—successfully, most of the time—to articulate in performance.

The constant reworking and the improvisational style of Dylan's vocal performances—coupled with his bands' ability to rework the arrangement of the song—have been a characteristic feature of the NET. Yet, what I would like to stress here is that this attitude is also crucial for the definition of Dylan's authenticity. The fact that a song can be sung in two subtly different ways on two different nights reinforces its "presentness" in the NET, when Dylan's voice is able to take his audience on a rhythmic and melodic rope-walk. It is an approach derived quite directly from the Grateful Dead's vision of their live act, but Dylan focused the change on his persona and his voice, rather than on the arrangement of the songs, as the quotations above clearly demonstrate. Of the Grateful Dead, David Pattie writes that the audience "provided the ultimate justification for the band's improvisatory style" (Pattie 2007, 67), and—quoting Blair Jackson's interview with Dead member Bob Weir—that Deadheads "let us do what we want musically, knowing that it's not always going to be great. And that's the best thing an audience can give me: the freedom to play what I feel." Dylan seems to have limited this freedom to his voice, which is projected against the background of more or less fixed arrangements. To some degree, every concert entails this sort of experimentation, which provides an unsafe environment for Dylan's vocal improvisations.

Although Dylan seems to owe much to the Grateful Dead, and he has played several songs that can be connected to the group (the arrangement of "Pretty Peggy-O," "Friend of the Devil," "Alabama Getaway," even "Not Fade Away" and his acoustic, lovely interpretation of "Two Soldiers," which Jerry Garcia recorded around the same time Dylan recorded his own version for *World Gone Wrong*),[5] there are also important differences. Although it is true that Dylan attempted to reshape and change his audience in terms of the creation of a community of knowledgeable fans, pretty much in the same way the Grateful Dead had done, his performances in the heyday of the NET stressed more the presentational side of performance at the expense of the participatory side, altering the relationship between artist, music, and community that characterizes the experience of fusion in a concert and that relies on the loosening of the boundaries between artist and audience. Dylan's choices of material and his innovative use of his singing voice created this set of distances that detached the artist as the subject of a presentation from his audience. Although many acts—the Grateful Dead chief among them—seem to interpret their touring activities as opportunities to renew their relationship with their fans, Dylan has constructed his aura in the NET around the tension between the availability of the artist year after year and the distance he puts between himself and his audience when on stage. This is in keeping with his belief that the songs, and not the myth of the artist, have to take center stage. Keith Negus makes an interesting point here. Although Dylan is "heir to the legacies of a type of social, communal music-making" that has been passed to him through folk and blues, his singing makes it almost impossible for the audience to participate, because "the new melodies and rhythms are often playing off and held in tension to the previously heard melodies and rhythms, whether it becomes tangible when people try to sing, or whether the audience become aware of it as the song unfolds against their memory of how the song last sounded" (Negus 2008, 153). Negus continues by giving a few examples of how the tangible connection with the audience is reaffirmed through singing along, most notably in a performance of "Like a Rolling Stone" in Glasgow 2004, according to Dylan "the best singing audience we ever had. We played that song a thousand times and nobody could sing it" (see also Negus 2007).

When this communion happens (in Glasgow 2004, Madrid 1995, or Tokyo 1997, all moments when "Like a Rolling Stone" reached this kind of performative convergence), the song itself becomes a conversation between Dylan and the audience. But a conversation always requires two voices that speak differently, engage each other, and work their way through to collaboration. Singing along with Dylan is an ambiguous sort of collaboration, for the performance of the song is constructed through the articulation of a double distance, between the song as performed (rearranged, re-phrased, made "local" through Dylan's approach to singing) and two different memories of the song: the song as it appears in the record, and—most importantly—the memory of the recorded artifact as it enters the performance through the intervention of the public. It is indeed the audience that sings the refrain of "Like a Rolling Stone" as close as possible to the way Dylan sang it in 1965, while the singer himself walks around this memory, beating a new pathway while never losing sight of the song, being constantly reminded by the public. In Madrid 1995, every verse is an exercise in improvisation, but no verse is exactly as it was or should be. The public, in this and other cases, stands in for the singer, allowing the singer to explore a different territory of the song, against memory, rather than performing a mere duplication of a cultural artifact that can be unproblematically recreated on the stage.

In performative terms, this approach defeats expectations. The NET, from this point of view, is not safe territory, as a Paul McCartney or a Bruce Springsteen show might be. Although Dylan has done this for most of his career (listen to "Like a Rolling Stone" in New Orleans 1981, for a remarkable example), the NET—with its focus on the value of performance—has accelerated this process, integrating unrecognizability as a peculiar, yet central, component of Dylan's aura and image. By stressing the perceived periphery of "Bob Dylan" (performer vs. songwriter, obscurities vs. hits, recognizability vs. unrecognizability) and bringing it to the center, Dylan frames other aspects of his relationship with the artist as a symbol, as part of a game of reconfiguration that can take place primarily only through performance, leaving the memorialized figure and its representational weight in the background. What becomes central, in other words, is a different set of assumptions about the artist that contribute in great part to the production of a peculiar "NET experience" (Lee Marshall writes of *consciousness*, but I would stay clear of the psychological underpinnings suggested by this term).

Dylan's authenticity can be easily found in these efforts, and it is, therefore, tightly bound to performance, enactment, and embodiment. The "authentic" Dylan of the 1990s and 2000s moves from this periphery to the center, challenging in fundamental ways the "authorized" view of the artist. Where one would expect an organ, there is a pedal steel guitar; where one would expect a solo acoustic song, "To Ramona" becomes a waltz made gentle by a bluegrass mandolin; where an orphan of the politically committed Dylan expects "Hurricane," he plays—as he often did in the early 2000s—"If Dogs Run Free" (from *New Morning*) as a jazzy vaudeville number. As long as change, not permanence, is reaffirmed as a marker of authenticity, Dylan's use of his repertoire and the performative twists to which his songbook is subjected help him transcend fixity, leading to unexpected places, which serves as a means to reconstruct the artist. This is, by all means, a constructed vision of authenticity that the artist has tried to make visible through the reworking of his own catalogue. Yet "constructed" does not mean "fake." It is, rather, a way for Dylan to move to the core of the American tradition, composite as it is, but also produced and experienced through many musical, generational, and racial peripheries (Mellers 1985). As Barry Shank has argued in an analysis of Dylan's "minstrelsy" (a lively subfield that has emerged following the release of Dylan's "*Love and Theft,*" a title lifted from Eric Lott's book on blackface minstrelsy: Lott 1995; Lott 2009; Nielsen 2009; Reginio 2009; Wilentz 2010, 261–286), "the history of American popular music is, in large part, a history of illusions and masks, of whites pretending to be black, of women pretending to be men, of sophisticated stage performers pretending to be rubes (and, of course, vice versa)" (Shank 2002, 98). Dylan's songs, as well as his other efforts throughout the period of the NET (from *Theme Time Radio Hour* to the movie *Masked and Anonymous*) achieve their goal of displaying authenticity, because they are repositioned—and reworked—in order to fit the idea of authenticity as the fabricated fantasy that connects the artist to a tradition, in a compression of social times (the past and the present, Dylan's past and the present) that simultaneously achieves timelessness.

In some sense, Dylan's songs as they are performed in the NET constitute another part of what Mick Cochrane has identified as Dylan's "buried autobiography" (Cochrane 2009). Although Cochrane is thinking about the songs that Dylan compiled for his radio program *Theme Time Radio Hour,* there is an important sense in which Dylan's own songs have attained an equal status: when performed on stage, detached from the circumstances of their original recording, they create a sense of distance that is at the same time visible and audible. Dylan's strategy of sonic revisionism has pointed consistently to this kind of outsiderness, only superficially resembling rock music. The primary characteristic of Dylan's sound, as it has been shaped in the NET since 1992, is the integration of a strong roots element achieved through the centrality of instruments that do not belong to the rock tradition he has been associated with. The sound of the NET has been shaped by the pedal steel, the lap steel guitar, and other instruments, like the banjo, the mandolin, the fiddle, the bouzouki, the standup bass, and sometimes the accordion (in 1993).[6] These are instruments that quite automatically connote "the past" and a roots-music tradition, that Dylan has explored since the *Basement Tapes,* but which, before the NET, rarely found a consistent expression on stage.[7] Indeed, this is almost the standard lineup of a string band, where banjo and fiddle were joined by bass, mandolins, and guitars.

As such, performances in the heyday of the NET (and to some extent still today) were often designed as a journey into American tradition (especially into the musical forms of American tradition) that was communicated both by Dylan's reinvented songs and by the covers he performed. The form of performance is as central as its content, because it is through form and the presentation on stage of an inclusive concept of "American folk song" that Dylan and the NET configure a narrative about collective memory. The borrowing of musical forms—and their presentation on stage—make a standard show from the NET immersed in tradition. Rock is just one of the elements of this dialogue with the audience about American music, and Dylan's effort in the NET (especially in the period from the mid-1990s to the early 2000s) seems to have been that of a bricoleur, continuously deconstructing the constitutive traditional elements of rock music, and reassembling them as a way to work with his songs.

The consequence of this attempt to present himself as an entrepreneur of memory, rather than as a passive object of collective memory, is quite important for the artist's reputation, because it brings an element of timelessness into the perception of what "Bob Dylan" does as a performer. By claiming (as he has always done) that tradition does not start with his own work, and by expressing on stage the fact that he belongs to a much broader culture of performing, Dylan has avoided in recent years the reproduction of a nostalgic vision that traps the artist in the cage of his own past, reaching other times, close and distant. Yet the timeless qualities that the most successful performances of the NET can produce and induce in the audience are paradoxically embedded in the historicity of performance. Dylan—by refusing (or forced by the changes in his voice) to perform the song "as in the record"—achieves a double objective through the here-and-now performance of a song: it situates the performance in the present, yet its traditional form and the traditional way of performing detaches the song from the present. Some of the songs Dylan covers speak of timelessness in the time of performance, because they represent a moment in this ongoing dialogue with the past and in most cases with the dead (Mance Lipscomb, Elizabeth Cotten, Lonnie Johnson, Leadbelly), but this objective can also be achieved by Dylan's own songs. Whether it is the 2008, banjo-driven arrangement of "It's Alright Ma" that attenuates the distances between this song, Dylan's "High Water," and the white blues of Clarence Ashley, Dock Boggs, and Roscoe Holcomb, or the direct appropriation and interpretation of this "memory palace," performances in the NET keep them together, in the double guise of traditionalized Dylan songs and modernized relics. By enacting tradition, as I will show in the next section, Dylan also avoids excessive memorialization and reclaims an autonomous space for the construction of his own memory.

Embodying Tradition and Dylan's Authenticity

The young Dylan said in the liner notes to his second album *The Freewheelin' Bob Dylan*: "I don't carry myself yet the way that Big Joe Williams, Woody Guthrie, Leadbelly and Lightnin' Hopkins have carried themselves. I hope to be able to someday, but they're older people. I sometimes am able to do it, but it happens, when it happens, unconsciously," suggesting that he had still a long way to go to reach the kind of authenticity that he saw in the singers of an older generation, black and white. With the release of his acoustic albums at the beginning of the 1990s, and until more recent days, some reviewers found that he had finally accomplished that dream: "[those old singers] are also counterpoints to Dylan's casually decadent rock star peers, who happily cater to their fans' demands. Unlike them, Dylan offers the audience only what he thinks they should want: an opportunity to see an artist work" (Wyman 2005). In most cases, and for much of the NET, this opportunity to see the artist at work was embedded in the projects I have described. He was defining a "New Dylan," who was able to bring tradition to the fore by carefully traditionalizing his approach and repertoire, a huge songbook where his own compositions walked hand in hand with (and sometimes perfectly indistinguishable from) songs that were older than he or anyone else who walked on earth: "Nothing seems to wake him up lately like a song someone else wrote—even more, a song that *no one else* wrote, songs that, like these, are obscure in origin and communally refined, that are not the work of a person (and are therefore *dust*), but of The People" (Lloyd 1993).

To some extent, even the songs that Dylan composed belong to this no-man's-land, where lyrics are lifted, appropriated, and transformed in their meaning by juxtaposition. Fellow songwriter Joni Mitchell has typecast Dylan as completely fake, voicing her contempt against Dylan's problematic technique of cutting up verses here and there, and pasting them into his own compositions: "Bob is not authentic at all. He's a plagiarist, and his name and voice are fake. Everything about Bob is a deception. We are like night and day, he and I" (Diehl 2010). In Mitchell's view, inauthenticity is connected to insincerity, and she charges them both with moral value, echoing a widespread conception of art, according to which—in critic Alex Neill's words—"one way in which a work of art may be inauthentic is in virtue of being insincere, of expressing and articulating sentiments which are or were not in fact those of the artist" (Neill 1999, 197). Joni Mitchell's notion of authenticity is—paradoxically —the long-term outcome of Dylan's efforts in the 1960s, to draw a neat line between the individual and the collective, between the songwriter as the bearer of individuality and the folk tradition from which he wanted to distance himself. This notion of authenticity seems to overlap with original- ity, and Mitchell values the latter and takes it as the only marker of authenticity. An authentic artist, it seems, is one who produces his own work and can only be evaluated as long as he and his work carry the mark of originality. This is not how Bob Dylan works, because he has always had—to quote David Yaffe—a "committee of muses" by his side (Yaffe

2011, 96). Yet the lifting, the citationism, the premodern and postmodern attitude toward joining couplets that can be old as the blues and as original as Dylan, has been (and has increasingly become) a trademark working practice through which Dylan incorporates and broadens tradition.[8]

There is more than a semantic convergence, or for that matter total overlapping of lines that cross social times and contexts. Where can the line "If you ever go to Houston you better walk right" be located beyond any doubt? In "Midnight Special" or in a song credited to Dylan? Does the line "the cuckoo is a pretty bird she warbles as she fly" take on extra effects when we hear it sung by Clarence Ashley or as a part of "High Water"? An excess of fragmentation deconstructs songs and performances as they were originally perceived and takes (borrows) from the past to create new surroundings for lines, couplets, and sonic elements, crossing the boundaries between social times and defying any perceivable separation between the past and the present. Dylan was familiar with these techniques even before the postmodern infatuation with citation: "Lord, the whole country, man, is overflowed" and "crash on the levee, mama, water's gonna overflow" can make sense only through juxtaposition, once one is able to walk around the web of references, mysteries, and traditions that Dylan incorporates in his songwriting.

These are lyrics from Patton's "High Water Everywhere" (from his Grafton sessions, at the dawn of the collapse of 1929) and Dylan's "Down in the Flood," a song from the *Basement Tapes*, and, thus, a song that is incorporated into Dylan's canon both as evidence of his creativity, and as one of the first instances of his recommitment to tradition, as Greil Marcus remarked in his "revisionist" account of the importance of the *Basement Tapes*. Michael Gray, together with other Dylan scholars who focus excessively on lyrics at the expense of performance, would argue that Dylan stands in a peculiar position vis-à-vis the blues, "as near to that of the poet or composer (even to the critic) as to the rock and roll performer" (Gray 2000, 272). Yet, what is different between Charley Patton's words and Dylan's, if one reads them without any concern for authorship or prejudgment about Dylan's poetry, which usually accompany the interpretation of every Dylan song? Not much. It seems, on the contrary, that Dylan's game of appropriation and reworking favors a poetic of simplicity, adapting his songwriting to the process—largely anonymous and therefore outside the standards of creative sincerity and originality that construct our contemporary vision of authenticity—that is essential, as a writing and performative practice, to understanding the blues. Thus, the theme of the flood (Leeder and Wells 2009) that one can find in Dylan's work is less an individual reflection than a means to enter deeper and older traditions, where dead men come to life by the rewriting of their words, regardless of whether there is a thematic proximity, as in the case of Charlie Patton, or a more explicit reworking as he did with the music of Memphis Minnie and Kansas Joe McKoy, direct references for Dylan's "The Levee's Gonna Break" (from *Modern Times,* 2006). When Dylan started alternating "Down in the Flood" and "Drifter's Escape" as openers in 1995, his voice sounded like it came from another land, not the land of rock. Rock was there in the arrangement, the structure of the song, the embellishments of John Jackson's guitar, but Dylan's voice was out there and down home. The blues has always provided these escapes from Dylan's image, but increasingly this has happened from within his own songs. "Mississippi" (from *"Love and Theft"*) owes its lovely refrain, "Only one thing I did wrong, stayed in Mississippi one day too long" to the haunting chain gang blues song, "Rosie," which Alan Lomax recorded in prison in the late 1940s. "High Water," a pastiche that is constructed almost as if to sound as ancient as America itself, is a vortex in which Dylan and the listener get caught by the line "I'll wake up in the morning I believe I'll dust my broom," a line that in itself is a journey back in time to visit the ghosts of Elmore James, Robert Lockwood, Robert Johnson, and Kokomo Arnold. Love and theft, indeed.

Entertaining this sort of dialogue is what constitutes Dylan's authenticity, both on record and in performance. The "deliberate archaism" (Wilentz 2010, 308) of song and performance is a form of engagement with memory, a strategy for achieving timelessness, but also a means to distance Dylan from the present. On stage, Dylan's nineteenth-century clothes add to the impression of temporal estrangement, as Dylan's "faces" try to achieve a sort of precarious connection with each other. Archaisms are strengthened, rather than bracketed out in records, as a curiosity that testifies to

Dylan's fascination with old-time music, by Dylan's implicit invitation to his listeners to seek the hidden gems in his songs and reconstruct the references that inhabit them, and by the incorporation of a broader musical tradition in his shows. In later years, the electric rhythm and blues of the 1950s has given shape to many of the songs Dylan has performed on stage (especially the ones from *Modern Times* and *Together through Life*), whereas, at the turn of the millennium, the Southern tradition of white gospel, bluegrass, and hillbilly music seemed to be the safest environment for Dylan's traveling show. Whether they are musical phrases, stolen because they have been previously loved, or the hundreds of covers he has played during the NET, these dialogic references create a different memory than the one that is constructed around Bob Dylan. They can come from any station in the long musical journey of contemporary Western culture, but hardly from the fixed image of Dylan that resonates in arenas other than the NET (which is usually a synthesis of Dylan the folksinger and Dylan the electric songwriter of the mid-1960s, two personae that have by now achieved a positive valence that has silenced all the controversies that characterized those periods and Dylan's rise to fame).

For an artist who individualized folk music by claiming his right to march to the beat of his own drummer, this turn to a traditionalized vision of Dylan and to the incorporation of tradition means simultaneously going backward and moving forward, in both cases not staying where he would be expected to be as an iconic artist. Whether Dylan's achieved *timelessness*—a term that seems to characterize so many recent analyses of his work and figure—is an intentional cultural project or not, it would make very little sense without the parallel performative "timelessness" that has become a distinctive trait of the NET. True, all major rock stars—especially those who have survived the 1960s—yearn to "stop time," and, accordingly, they frame their shows as a musical retrospective down memory lane or to bring repetition of their successful formula to perfection. Even in those cases where an artist plays effectively with traditional elements—like in Springsteen's efforts with the Seeger Session Band—they are confined to projects that are separated from the main focus of the reinforcement of a mythology that has its roots in rock music. Dylan, on the contrary, has distanced himself from these domestications of the tradition he refers to, start-ing from the way he carries himself on stage, as a cowboy who could have toured with Bob Wills in the 1930s, or as a dressed-up gambler who—amazingly—could have found his place on a Mississippi paddle steamer.

This effort to portray a new image of Dylan that seems to be constructed out of a bricolage that holds together musical forms and stylistic elements has grown to reach a synthesis between the distant series of pasts Dylan claims to be a for-gotten musical legacy and his own work. In 1999 and 2000, Dylan often played two to three covers per show ("Not Fade Away" being the standard encore in many shows). "Not Fade Away" was rock from a distant age, but he decided to open with songs that predated rock and roll. Standard openers in 1999, 2000, and 2001 were the Stanley Brothers' "I Am the Man, Thomas," the traditional "Roving Gambler," Elizabeth Cotten's "Oh, Babe It Ain't No Lie," or "Duncan and Brady." In 2000, gospel songs began to appear as his openers: "Some-body Touched Me," or "Hallelujah, I'm Ready to Go." Shows that start in this way create from the beginning a double experience of estrangement from the image of the artist, one that deals with established representations about Dylan and his artistic achievements, and the other with the experience of the concert itself. Any of the songs—many of them covers—that Dylan used to enrich his show in that period, with their string-band, semi-acoustic arrangements and the narratives they told, could have been played anytime between 1930 and the 2000s, but hardly by Dylan during his 1960s hip period. The band and the staging reinforce the feeling that—despite Dylan's presence—what is being played is music out of time. The performance of these songs—at least in the period be-tween 1999 and 2001—was organized in such a way that the experience of Dylan as an active organizer of memory would be a part of the shows. For the first time since 1966, Dylan scripted his shows by separating the acoustic set from the electric one. The covers of traditional or traditional sound-ing material opened the concert, and sometimes marked the end of the acoustic set. Dylan's songs were encapsulated between these songs, strengthening the impression that they, too, belonged to tradition. Some of them, actually, gained new strength from their juxtaposition to the covers Dylan played. "Ballad of Hollis Brown," for example, reveals its roots only when it resides close to songs like "The Long Black Veil," a country standard that was written to sound like it came from outside of time. "To Ramona" and "Boots of Spanish Leather" reclaim their place in the years of the folk revival when they are interchangeable with Elizabeth Cotten's "Shake Sugaree." Dylan has used the experience of the NET in the years when it worked most effectively to attenuate the distances between him and his lexicon to build the contemporary image of Bob Dylan.

In some sense, all these efforts—meant to reveal the successful appropriation of a tradition—are a trademark of Dylan's practices of authenticity. The shows of the NET have been an extension of Dylan's effort to construct a reputation as a mediator of a cultural tradition that shapes authenticity in a way that precedes the affirmation of cultural industry, the subjectivity of the author, and the definition of individual artistry. In some respects, both the NET and the other activities that have involved Dylan over the past twenty years rework the canon of the folk process, unveiling roots (in the concerts and in the records), updating them, and circulating them to the audience, which, through this performed statement about authenticity, can align with a new vision of Dylan that is free of the constraints imposed by the residue of the 1960s narrative. Without this broad set of cultural references that cross time and link diverse elements of American vernacular music, Dylan's reputation could hardly be different from the one he has challenged since the beginning of the NET. This authenticity, however, had to be constructed in a very practical and visible way, and the NET has provided the setting and the stage for this performance of authenticity. Everything in Dylan, today, hints and speaks to authenticity, from his stage persona to —paradoxically—his ragged and worn voice that is so distant from the stereotype the audience has constructed about it.

The dynamics of artistic reputation have served to offer a vision of Dylan where collective memory is embodied by the artist, and yet it is not the collective memory *of* the artist but a broader narrative of memorialization, where the artist is involved in a work that challenges fundamental aspects of the iconic vision of Dylan that have become part of public memory. In some sense, the NET has provided an opportunity for the production of a memory from the periphery, which

Dylan has sought—successfully—to bring to the center. Dylan stands not for his past, nor simply for his work. More than ever, he seems to stand as a social symbol that speaks simultaneously of his past and the past of the culture he has unwillingly represented over more than fifty years, to which he has returned. Until his next unexpected move.

Notes

1. Among them, Leonard Cohen, Van Morrison, Warren Zevon, and Johnny Cash, whose work has been covered by Dylan in many performances of the Never Ending Tour. Yet the (mostly) American landscape that Dylan explored during the Never Ending Tour was considerably larger and included anybody from Chuck Berry to Elizabeth Cotten, the Rolling Stones and The Clash, Tim Hardin and a good number of country songwriters. For an almost complete catalogue of Dylan's covers, see Barker (2008).

2. After the first box set to appear in the *Bootleg Series*, which was a retrospective of Dylan's career through rarities, demos, and bootleg recordings, half of the releases cover the period between 1961 and 1966: There have been two live concerts (at the Royal Philharmonic Hall and at the Free Trade Hall in Manchester), a collection of demos recorded originally for copyright reasons (The Leeds and Witmark Demos), and the soundtrack for *No Direction Home*. The remaining volumes document selected songs from the first Rolling Thunder Revue and Dylan's output over the past twenty years.

3. Four songs circulate among collectors, and "Miss the Mississippi and You" (another cover, originally by Jimmie Rodgers, has been officially released on *The Bootleg Series 8—Tell Tale Signs*). "I found myself writing this song, this story, this long piece of vomit about twenty pages long, and out of it I took 'Like a Rolling Stone' and made it a single." Martin Bronstein interviewed Dylan for the Canadian Broadcasting Corporation on February 20, 1966, when Dylan was playing in Montreal during the North-American leg of his world tour. The passage is taken from the tape of the interview, which circulates in the fan community.

4. Dylan also did a short tour with the Grateful Dead in 1987, and he has often referred to that experience as one that changed his approach to live music. It is no surprise, then, that after touring with the Dead, Dylan started to build his own show, incorporating ideas that were at the center of the Grateful Dead's vision of performance, like the enhancement of multiple attendance and the ever-changing setlists.

5. From this point of view, Dylan is right when he claims that there was a Never Ending Tour but it ended with the departure of guitarist G. E. Smith. Starting in 1992 and for the following two decades, Dylan's sound on stage was quite consistent, but it never featured the tight rock band (drums, bass, and two guitars) that he fronted during the first period of the NET. Accordingly, his sound has moved from rock to a more accentuated roots sound, heavily influenced by blues, bluegrass, and country.

6. There were *hints* though, like Dylan's appearance with The Band at the Woody Guthrie memorial concert in 1968, the inclusion of violin, pedal steel guitar, and mandolin during the Rolling Thunder Revue, and the Appalachian autoharp that one of Dylan's backing singers used to accompany him during the Musical Retrospective tour in the fall of 1980.

7. Nor does the controversy seem to be limited to Dylan's songs. In September 2011, many noted that the paintings that Dylan was exhibiting at the Gagosian Gallery in New York were, indeed, "citations" of famous photographs.

8. The official release of the *Basement Tapes* (1975) bears just a pale resemblance to Dylan's outburst of creativity in the months following the famous motorcycle accident and his retirement in Woodstock. For research purposes, I have used mainly bootleg recordings, *Genuine Basement Tapes,* and organ player Garth Hudson's reels, which have recently resurfaced. When they are released officially—hopefully as a multiple-CD box set—these line recordings will add significantly to our comprehension of Dylan's music in the 1960s and will prove to be evidence of the fact that Dylan's electric period should be considered as a present-oriented departure from his longtime obsession with the core project of adaptation and change of American roots music tradition.

◇

Conclusions

That Dylan is likely to make an unexpected move (even at seventy, even when out there some people may think he's over the hill and past his prime) is part of the huge reputation he has built over the past fifty years. After all, nobody expected Dylan's first Christmas record (just another journey in the American musical landscape), and nobody thought—back then—than Dylan would be touring so restlessly for decades. As I write these conclusions, in November 2011, I have just come back from a road trip in Italy, to attend three shows in the Never Ending Tour. Even if these trips are less exciting than they were, say, in 1994–1995 or 1999–2001, they are still part of my personal and highly solipsistic experience of Bob Dylan. Indeed, I doubt that my decision to study Dylan with a dominant focus on performance would have been the same had I been less than a dedicated fan, and had the NET experience not been so crucial in shaping my relationship to Dylan's work.

When I started this project in 2008, however, I was moved by something more than fandom that struck me as a social scientist and that informed the early drafts of this book, especially what became the analysis of Dylan's trajectory from folk revivalism to rock (Chapters 1 and 2). Then, what was originally thought to be an idea for a paper turned into a book, the more I realized that the relationship between Dylan and performance is one of the most excellent case studies I could find about the interaction between the construction of artistic reputation and symbolic action. As such, it touches much deeper meanings about culture and the symbolization of relevant figures than I had envisaged at the beginning.

In taking this direction, I was influenced by an internal turn in what could pompously be labeled "Dylan studies," which has gained momentum in recent years. Although biographers and fans have long been interested in the details of Dylan's rise to fame, cultural history and the sociology of culture have only recently started to become interested in the dynamics of the production of Dylan's artistic reputation. The adoption of this new approach—epitomized by two of the most important books that have been published in recent years, Lee Marshall's *Bob Dylan: The Never Ending Star* and Sean Wilentz's collection of essays *Bob Dylan in America* —has meant a shift from the study of Dylan's works, and especially the lyrics of his songs, to the investigation of the social context and the processes in which this great oeuvre has been produced, circulated, and recognized as a peculiar contribution to American and global popular culture. This cultural-historical cum sociological turn has taken place in the recent context of the canonization of Bob Dylan as a founding figure for contemporary popular music, and in a sense it has contributed to it from a scholarly perspective. As much as they have contributed to our understanding of Dylan and his work, these authors, and many others, from Mike Marqusee's (2003) interpretation of Dylan's political role in the sixties and beyond to Greil Marcus, from Keith Negus to Christopher Ricks, have also been involved in the process of bringing Dylan's reputation outside the boundaries of popular culture and making it academically respectable.

Yet, even though these efforts have contributed greatly to our understanding of Dylan, the context that has favored his rise to fame, and some of the reasons why his work appeals to a large number of fans, they have fallen short of providing a truly sociological description (thick in detail and meaning) of the particularities of Dylan's trajectory, nor was this their primary purpose.

In attempting to offer a sociological description of some key moments in Dylan's career, I have tried to flesh out the complexity of the interaction between how an individual artist presents himself in public (and in this case on the stage) and the dynamics of reputation-making. This is not only a consequence of the system of relations and interactions in which he is embedded, but also a construct that relies on the accessibility of deep meanings, socially distributed and communicatively made available, that create the "social place" of artists—and prominent individuals—in our modern and postmodern society.

What many studies of celebrity, fame, and artistic reputation (mostly at the crossroads of cultural studies and cultural history) try to achieve is a balance between the idea that celebrities are ideologically constructed and that the production of iconic figures serves a symbolic function for various communities or audiences. Although these are long-standing alternatives in social theory (symbolic figures hide the dynamics of ideology-work in society, or they are fundamental for orienting public perception and produce integration into wider communities of belief and feelings), it seems that effective work on the dynamics of the creation of artists as social symbols needs to move toward an integration of the two perspectives, as the only possible way to achieve a high degree of multidimensionality in the analysis of reputations. Thus, the lives and works of many popular musicians have been translated into the vocabulary of cultural studies, the sociology of culture, and cultural history: we have had —to name some of the most relevant contributions to this historical sociology of icons—the cultural history of John Lennon (Makela 2004); Robert Johnson and Latina singer Selena have become social texts upon which mythographies have been written (Paredez 2009; Schroeder 2004); Dusty Springfield has been understood as an interpreter and entrepreneur in a transnational, transracial game able to bridge the two sides of the Atlantic and import black soul to white England (Randall 2008). The list goes on, and it testifies to a paradigm shift in the way we write and think about artists and the sociological conditions of their emergence and management.

The process by means of which we "create" and "make" artists and popular icons is a collective one, and it involves in interaction (and competition, as we have seen) artists, audiences, and mediators. Before any broadcasting of an individual reputation to a public, in fact, a center of production must be involved. Artists are not isolated in the creation of their own reputation to the audience, and they must rely on more ordinary arrangements of creators and mediators of their reputation, what Gary Fine (2001) calls "reputational entrepreneurs," those socially powerful figures, placed in strategic positions in a network, who have the capacity to produce reputation-work. Such constructivist vision contrasts greatly with commonsense ideas that see Dylan as the sole creator of his reputation and—partially—of his art. I have decided to look at this idea of Bob Dylan, his identity as an artist, and his role as one of the many *representations* that compete in the public space for recognition, rather than as a "reality" per se. The point has been, in other words, to reconstruct the representational and institutional trajectory of Bob Dylan in such a way as to highlight the role played by the many forces, actors, and circumstances that have contributed to shape his current, iconic status.

By pointing out that Dylan's career trajectory would have been very different (and possibly there might hardly have been a career) without a network of relationships, where Pete Seeger, Albert Grossman, Izzy Young, singers, and writers, interacted and competed, I have tried to illustrate both the complexity and the relative unpredictability of the local turning points that punctuated Dylan's rise to fame and the reputation-projects that were associated with this career trajectory. Dylan's perceived charisma and the exceptionality of his "genius" make sense not in a realistic way, but because, in the fixation of these defining traits of his work and reputation, we see interactions and social activities.

On the other hand, the charismatic reading is something to be explained, rather than something that can provide a ready-made explanation of Dylan's reputation. It must be described in two senses that often overlap: first, its emergence has to be analyzed and brought back to a more sociological understanding, according to which Dylan's charisma is not an individual feature but the result of processes of interaction and recognition; second, it has to be approached as a valuable strategic resource that Dylan has exploited over the years to project his many images to his audiences, making them more or less consistent and attuned to a "liminal" and "creative" view of the artist that could encompass in a more or less coherent whole the vicissitudes and the ups and downs of an otherwise complex career.

This latter sense goes straight to the core of Dylan's attempt to define a social space where authenticity, perceived originality, and the presentation of the artist could interact. The more Dylan became an iconic figure, the more he was able to silence (though not obliterate) the conditions that had made the emergence of his star image possible and reinforce the public discourses and narratives about the originality of his genius, and his natural born authenticity. It was in such a context that both Dylan's mystery and his visibility as one of the most prominent artists of the past five decades set in. Dylan's mystery—as I have tried to show—is the mystery of liminal figures, those who belong to many worlds and in the end do not belong anywhere else than the space and time they inhabit at the moment, like all figures that change the rules of their game. Dylan's visibility has made—counterintuitively—this mystery accessible, whether it was through the reproduction of his image, his songs, or his live performances.

My contention in this book has been that it is quite surprising that the understanding of Dylan's charismatic reputation has neglected performance and public presentation for so long, except for rare instances, which—however—did not rely on performance studies or on the sociology of symbolic action. Performances are ephemeral, temporally bounded, witnessed by concrete rather than by imagined communities. But, on the other hand, they are also the social site—a potentially risky and contentious social site—where the artist as an icon is required to embody and communicate his iconicity, opening himself to the embrace of the crowd but also to the audience's critique, called into a game of collaboration in the definition of the artist that can result in the clash between representations and presentations, between what Dylan is supposed to look and sound like and how he carries himself on the stage.

A few days ago (as I write in November 2011) I was chatting with two young fans in their early twenties. Both of them were at their first Dylan concert. The guy was utterly disappointed; the girl enthusiastic beyond imagination. And I tried to explain to them that there was nothing new in their totally opposite receptions. Dylan would not be Dylan if he had not gone through this fragmentation of his audience since the beginning, and that was probably one of the reasons for his appeal. People typecast him as a fake in 1963, booed him in 1965, rejected his faith in 1979, did not recognize his songs in 1991; and, in any of those moments, people were deeply enamored with those deconstructions.

As long as there is controversy, Dylan will be alive and well, familiar in the feeling of disturbing familiarity that he is still able to inspire in his audience.

Yet, performance works in a more nuanced way. It not only provides the opportunity for the audience to see and evaluate the artist, but it also represents the setting in which Dylan has often made a public statement about his positioning as an artist. In this book, I have used as a common thread Richard Peterson's notion of "hard-core authenticity," a strategy that Dylan seems to have used since the beginning of his career. Contrary to Peterson, however, I have highlighted the cultural work that is involved in the production and circulation, not to mention reception, of this type of authenticity. As a cultural sociologist, whatever that might mean, I have tried to grasp a potential contradiction in Dylan's case, that he still works (and he is still perceived) as a hard-core artist, while being safely positioned and canonized at the center of popular music. Dylan's star image—surprisingly for an artist of his stature—has been created, circulated, and reinforced mostly in a movement from the periphery to the center, at the same time domesticating the periphery and "centralizing" it. This particular trajectory would have been hardly possible in the absence of performances, those micro-events that involve the presentation of the artist's take on the center–periphery dichotomy and that are used in turn as occasions for the redefinition of those boundaries. Murray the K's announcement that one of Dylan's performances was "not folk, not rock" but "a new thing called Dylan" fits well with this idea of the breaking and collapsing of the established boundaries of genre and also of the boundaries of performance.

To a sociologist, the center–periphery alternative is often a normative one (Shils 1975), which involves prescriptions about how life has to be, in its moral and institutional arrangements. Yet it also involves the very symbolic activities through which the boundaries and the content of what stands on either side of the boundaries are defined. Yet, what happens indeed when those activities are boundary-crossing, rather than boundary-making? This seems to be one of the most insightful sociological suggestions that one can make out of Dylan's case. When Dylan works, whether in the Rolling Thunder Revue or in one of the many nights of the Never Ending Tour, he places himself in a musical and cultural periphery; yet Dylan is also positioned at the center of our ideas about popular culture. One would think performances can work as a way to synthesize these two contrasting visions. And yet, Dylan's fascination as a performing artist lies mostly in the constant affirmation of the value of periphery and the role performance plays in hinting to the public that this is where the artist should always belong. Without these stratified peripheries experienced in the here-and-now of performance, there would be no authenticity for Dylan.

The authentic Dylan, thus, reveals himself through performance, and at this point whether a performance is good or bad matters less than the very effort to be "authentic." I have seen an authentic Dylan barking through the lines of "Tomorrow Is a Long Time" in 2008 (my favorite love song torn to pieces on a November night in New York) and so intoxicated in 1992 that he was hardly able to remember the words to "All along the Watchtower." And yet the feeling that what I was seeing was an authentic artist struggling to give an authentic performance never went away. Which leads to my final point, and to the conclusion of this book. It is a most striking contradiction that Dylan's authenticity is constructed precisely through these feelings that create a connection to the artist, whereas his image is constructed often through the aseptic dissection of his words, lyrics, and verses. Performances, indeed, reveal the emotional side of authenticity, and the link between the artist and the audience is more often than not an affective one, effervescent and contingent because it can find its way only in performance.

This is probably the reason why fans return to Dylan even when they know the melodic rope-walking, the adventurous phrasing, the exciting setlists are long gone, unlikely to reappear now that Dylan is aging. Yet there are still moments when Dylan does it again, and they can be witnessed only if one is there, on a particular night and at a particular moment. A few days ago (November 14, 2011), I heard my third "Desolation Row" in five days. "They're selling postcards of the hanging." Something special was beginning to take shape. "They are painting the passports brown." Dylan's voice was going back in time. "The beauty parlor is filled with sailors, the circus is in town." For three or four verses, including Cinderella who puts her hand in her back pocket Bette Davis style (a line that at that particular moment was very special to me), Dylan nailed the song, he knew it, and was probably too scared to bring the song to its conclusion, leading his words to a wreck that bore no resemblance to the improvisational tour de force I had just witnessed. It could have happened only in performance. People around me were probably too bored, disappointed by his current voice, distracted by the loud volume to notice it. To me, it all made sense. I smiled and turned the other way.

◆

References

Alexander, J. C. 2004. "Cultural Pragmatics: Social Performance between Ritual and Strategy." *Sociological Theory* 22(4): 527–573.

Appelrouth, S. 2011. "Boundaries and Early Jazz: Defining a New Music." *Cultural Sociology* 5(2): 225–242.

Auslander, P. 1998. "Seeing Is Believing: Live Performance and the Discourse of Authenticity in Rock Culture." *Literature and Psychology* 44(4): 1–26.

———. 2004. "Performance Analysis and Popular Music: A Manifesto." *Contemporary Theatre Review* 14(1): 1–13.

Bakhtin, M. 1981. *The Dialogic Imagination.* Ed. M. Holquist. Austin: University of Texas Press.

Bareiss, W. 2010. "Middlebrow Knowingness in 1950s San Francisco: The Kingston Trio, Beat Counterculture, and the Production of 'Authenticity.'" *Popular Music and Society* 33(1): 9–33.

Barker, D. 2008. *The Songs He Didn't Write: Bob Dylan under the Influence.* New Malden, UK: Chrome Dreams.

Bauldie, J., ed. 1988. *The Ghost of Electricity: Bob Dylan's 1966 World Tour.* N.P.

———, ed. 1992. *Wanted Man: In Search of Bob Dylan.* London: Penguin.

Becker, H. 1982. *Art Worlds.* Chicago: University of Chicago Press.

Benjamin, W. 2008. *The Work of Art in the Age of Its Technological Reproducibility, and Other Writings on Media.* Cambridge, MA: Belknap Press of Harvard University Press.

Bluestein, G. 1994. *Poplore: Folk and Pop in American Culture.* Amherst: University of Massachusetts Press.

Bourdieu, P. 1993. *The Field of Cultural Production.* New York: Columbia University Press.

Bowden, B. 1982. *Performed Literature.* Bloomington: Indiana University Press.

Brackett, D. 2002. "[In Search of] Musical Meaning: Genres,

Categories, and Crossover." In *Popular Music Studies,* edited by D. Hesmondhalgh and K. Negus, 65–83: London: Arnold.

Brinkley, J. 2009. "Bob Dylan's America." *Rolling Stone,* May 14.

Brocken, M. 2003. *The British Folk Revival 1944–2002.* Aldershot, UK: Ashgate.

Brooks, P. 1976. *The Melodramatic Imagination: Balzac, Henry James, Melodrama, and the Mode of Excess.* New Haven, CT: Yale University Press.

Burns, J. 2008. *Series of Dreams: The Vision Songs of Bob Dylan.* Kirkcudbright, UK: Glen Murray Publishing.

Byrne, J. P. 2004. "The Genesis of Whiteface in Nineteenth-Century American Popular Culture." *Melus* 29(3/4): 133–149.

Cantwell, R. 1996. *When We Were Good: The Folk Revival.* Cambridge, MA: Harvard University Press.

Champlin, C. 1965. "Folks Pay Homage to Dylan." *Los Angeles Times,* September 6.

Child, B. 2009. "Raised in the Country, Working in the Town: Temporal and Spatial Modernisms in Bob Dylan's 'Love and Theft.'" *Popular Music and Society* 32(2): 199–210.

Clayman, S. 1993. "Booing: The Anatomy of a Disaffiliative Response." *American Sociological Review* 58(1): 110–130.

Clayton, S. 2009. "Not from Nowhere: Identity and Aspiration in Bob Dylan's Hometown." In *Highway 61 Revisited: Bob Dylan's Road from Minnesota to the World,* edited by C. J. Sheehy and T. Swiss, 25–38. Minneapolis: University of Minnesota Press.

Cochrane, M. 2009. "Bob Dylan's Lives of the Poets: Theme Time Radio Hour as Buried Autobiography." In *Highway 61 Revisited: Bob Dylan's Road from Minnesota to the World,* edited by C. J. Sheehy and T. Swiss, 133–139. Minneapolis: University of Minnesota Press.

Cohen, R. D. 2002. *Rainbow Quest: The Folk Music Revival and American Society, 1940–1970.* Amherst: University of Massachusetts Press.

Coleman, R. 1965. "A Beatle-Size Fever without the Screams." *Melody Maker,* May 8.

Corcoran, N., ed. 2003. "Do You, Mr. Jones?" *Bob Dylan with the Poets and the Professors.* London: Pimlico.

Cott, J., ed. 2006. *Dylan on Dylan.* London: Hodder and Stoughton.

Dawbarn, B. 1965. "Thank Goodness We Won't Get This Six-Minute Bob Dylan Single in Britain." *Melody Maker,* August 7.

Day, A. 1988. *Jokerman: Reading the Lyrics of Bob Dylan.* Oxford, UK: Blackwell.

DeGloma, T. 2010. "Awakenings: Autobiography, Memory, and the Social Logic of Personal." *Sociological Forum* 25(3): 519–540.

Denisoff, S. 1965. "Dylan: Hero or Villain?" *Broadside* 58, May 15.

DeNora, T. 1995. *Beethoven and the Construction of Genius: Musical Politics in Vienna, 1792–1803*. Berkeley: University of California Press.

DeNora, T., and H. Mehan. 1993. "Genius: A Social Construction." In *Constructing the Social*, edited by J. Kitsuse and T. Sarbin, 157–173. London: Sage.

De Turk, D. A., and A. Poulin, eds. 1967. *The American Folk Scene: Dimensions of the Folk Music Revival*. New York: Dell.

Diehl, T. 2010. "It's a Joni Mitchell Concert, Sans Joni." *Los Angeles Times*, April 22.

DiMaggio, P. 1987. "Classification in Art." *American Sociological Review* 52(4): 440–455.

Duffett, M. 2009. "'We Are Interrupted by Your Noise': Heckling and the Symbolic Economy of Popular Music Stardom." *Popular Music and Society* 32(1): 37–57.

Dunlap, J. 2005. "Understanding Bob and Renaldo." In *20 Years of Isis: Bob Dylan Anthology Volume 2*, edited by D. Barker, 201–217. New Malden, UK: Chrome Dreams.

Durkheim, E. 1995. *The Elementary Forms of Religious Life*. New York: The Free Press.

Dylan, B. 2004a. *Lyrics 1962–2001*. New York: Simon and Schuster.

———. 2004b. *Chronicles Volume One*. New York: Simon and Schuster.

Elliott, R. 2009. "The Same Distant Places: Bob Dylan's Poetics of Place and Displacement." *Popular Music and Society* 32(2): 249–270.

Elwood, P. 1979. "Bob Dylan: His Born-Again Show's a Real Drag." *San Francisco Examiner*, November 2.

Englehart, M. 1999. "Maximum Bob." *Guitar World*, March.

Eyerman, R., and A. Jamison. 1998. *Music and Social Movements: Mobilizing Traditions in the Twentieth Century*. Cambridge: Cambridge University Press.

Fabbri, F. 1982. "A Theory of Popular Music Genres: Two Applications." In *Popular Music Perspectives*, edited by D. Horn and P. Tagg, 52–81. Göteborg, Sweden: A. Wheaton.

Farley, C. J. 2001. "Legend of Dylan." *Time*, September 17.

Filene, B. 2000. *Romancing the Folk: Public Memory and American Roots Music*. Chapel Hill: University of North Carolina Press.

Fine, G. A. 2001. *Difficult Reputations: Collective Memories of the Evil, Inept, and Controversial*. Chicago: University of Chicago Press.

Frith, S. 1996. *Performing Rites: On the Value of Popular Music*. Cambridge, MA: Harvard University Press.

Garfinkel, H. 1956. "Conditions of Successful Degradation Ceremonies." *The American Journal of Sociology* 5: 420–424.

Giamo, B. 2011, "Bob Dylan's Protean Style." Paper presented at the "Refractions of Bob Dylan" Conference, Vienna (Austria), May 19–21.

Gill, A. 2011. *Bob Dylan: The Stories behind the Songs 1962–1969.* London: Carlton Books.

Gill, A., and K. Odegard. 2005. *A Simple Twist of Fate: Bob Dylan and the Making of "Blood on the Tracks."* Cambridge, MA: Da Capo.

Gilmore, M. 2001a. "Bob Dylan." *Rolling Stone,* November 22.

———. 2001b. "Bob Dylan." *Rolling Stone,* December 6–13.

Gilmour, M. J. 2004. *Tangled Up in the Bible: Bob Dylan and Scripture.* New York: Continuum.

———. 2011. *The Gospel According to Bob Dylan: The Old, Old Story for Modern Times.* Louisville, KY: Westminster John Knox Press.

Gray, M. 2000. *Song and Dance Man III: The Art of Bob Dylan.* London: Continuum.

Griffin, S. 2010. *Shelter from the Storm: Bob Dylan's Rolling Thunder Years.* London: Jawbone Press.

Gundersen, E. 1995. "Dylan on Dylan, Unplugged, and the Birth of a Song." *USA Today,* May 5–7.

———. 2001. "Dylan is Positively on Top of His Game." *USA Today,* September 10.

Hajdu, D. 2001. *Positively 4th Street: The Lives and Times of Joan Baez, Bob Dylan, Mimi Baez Fariña and Richard Fariña.* New York: Picador.

Hale, G. E. 2011. *A Nation of Outsiders: How the White Middle Class Fell in Love with Rebellion in Postwar America.* Oxford: Oxford University Press.

Harvey, T. 2001. *The Formative Dylan: Transmission and Stylistic Influences 1961–1963.* Lanham, MD: Scarecrow Press.

Heine, S. 2009. *Bargainin' for Salvation: Bob Dylan, a Zen Master?* New York: Continuum.

Heylin, C. 1995. *Bob Dylan: The Recording Sessions 1960–1994.* New York: St. Martin's Press.

———. 2009. *Revolution in the Air: The Songs of Bob Dylan 1957–1973.* Chicago: Chicago Review Press.

Hilburn, R. 1980. "Bob Dylan Says He's Truly Born-Again," *Los Angeles Times,* November 23.

———. 2001. "How Does It Feel? Don't Ask," *Los Angeles Times,* September 16.

Hobsbawm, E., and T. Ranger, eds. 1983. *The Invention of Tradition.* Cambridge: Cambridge University Press.

Holmes, T. 2007. "Us and Them: America's Rock Reconquista." *Popular Music and Society* 30(3): 343–353.

Holt, F. 2007. *Genre in Popular Music.* Chicago: University of Chicago Press.

Howard, J. R., and J. M. Streck. 1999. *Apostles of Rock: The Splintered World of Contemporary Christian Music.* Lexington: University Press of Kentucky.

Hughes, K. 1980. "Interview." *The Dominion,* August 2.

Hyde, L. 1998. *Trickster Makes This World: Mischief, Myth, and Art.* New York: North Point Press.

Inglis, I. 1996. "Synergies and Reciprocities: The Dynamics of Musical and Professional Interaction between the Beatles and Bob Dylan." *Popular Music and Society* 20(4): 53–79.

———, ed. 2006. *Performance and Popular Music: History, Place, and Time.* Aldershot, UK: Ashgate.

Irwin, C. 2008. *Legendary Sessions: Bob Dylan—Highway 61 Revisited.* London: Flame Tree Publishing.

Jansen, R. S. 2007. "Resurrection and Appropriation: Reputational Trajectories, Memory Work, and the Political Use of Historical Figures." *American Journal of Sociology* 112(4): 953–1007.

Kauffman, W. 2011. *Woody Guthrie, American Radical.* Urbana: University of Illinois Press.

Kennedy, T. 2009. "Bob Dylan's 'Highway Shoes': The Hobo-Hero's Road through Modernity." *Intertexts* 13(1): 37–58.

Klapp, O. 1964. *Symbolic Leaders: Public Dramas and Public Men.* Chicago: Aldine.

Klein, J. 1999. *Woody Guthrie: A Life.* New York: Random House.

Kokay, L. 2003. *Songs of the Underground. A Collectors' Guide to the Rolling Thunder Revue 1975–6,* self-published publication.

Kupfer, D. 2001. "Long Time Passing: An Interview with Pete Seeger." *Whole Earth Magazine,* Spring.

Lamont, M., and V. Molnar. 2002. "The Study of Boundaries in the Social Sciences." *Annual Review of Sociology* 28:167–195.

Lang, G., and K. Lang. 2001(1990). *Etched in Memory: The Building and Survival of Artistic Reputation.* Urbana: University of Illinois Press.

Lee, C. P. 2004a. *Like a Bullet of Light. The Films of Bob Dylan.* London: Helter Skelter.

———. 2004b. *Like the Night (Revisited): Bob Dylan and the Road to the Manchester Free Trade Hall.* London: Helter Skelter.

———. 2009. "Like the Night: Reception and Reaction Dylan UK 1966." In *Highway 61 Revisited: Bob Dylan's Road from Minnesota to the World,* edited by C. J. Sheehy and T. Swiss, 78–83. Minneapolis: University of Minnesota Press.

Leeder, M., and I. Wells. 2009. "Dylan's Floods." *Popular Music and Society* 32(2): 211–227.

Lemert, C. 2003. *Muhammad Ali: Trickster in the Culture of Irony.* Oxford, UK: Polity.

Lethem, J. 2006. "The Genius of Bob Dylan." *Rolling Stone,* September 7.

Lindsey, H. 1970. *The Late Great Planet Earth.* Grand Rapids, MI: Zondervan.

Lloyd, R. 1993. "Endless Skyline." *L.A. Weekly,* December 17.

Lott, E. 1995. *Love and Theft: Blackface Minstrelsy and the American Working Class.* Oxford, UK: Oxford University Press.

———. 2009. "Love and Theft." In *The Cambridge Companion to Bob Dylan,* edited by K. J. H. Dettmar, 167–173. Cambridge: Cambridge University Press.

MacColl, E., P. Ochs, et al. 1967. "Topical Songs and Folksingers 1965: A Symposium." In *The American Folk Scene,* edited by D. De Turk and A. Poulin, 150–166. New York: Dell.

MacDonald, S. 2009. "From Underground to Multiplex: An Interview with Todd Haynes." *Film Quarterly* 62(3): 54–64.

Makela, J. 2004. *John Lennon Imagined: Cultural History of a Rock Star.* New York: Peter Lang.

Marcus, G. 2006. *Like a Rolling Stone: Bob Dylan at the Crossroads.* New York: PublicAffairs.

———. 2010. *Bob Dylan. Writings 1968–2010.* New York: PublicAffairs.

Marqusee, M. 2003. *Wicked Messenger: Bob Dylan and the 1960s.* New York: Seven Stories Press.

Marshall, L. 2006. "Bob Dylan, Newport Folk Festival, July 25, 1965." In *Performance and Popular Music: History, Time, and Place,* edited by I. Inglis, 16–27. Aldershot, UK: Ashgate.

———. 2007. *Bob Dylan: The Never Ending Star.* Oxford, UK: Polity.

Masur, L. 2007. "Famous Long Ago: Bob Dylan Revisited." *American Quarterly* 59(1): 165–177.

McGregor, C., ed. 1990. *Bob Dylan: The Early Years—A Retrospective.* New York: Da Capo.

Mellers, W. 1985. *A Darker Shade of Pale: A Backdrop to Bob Dylan.* Oxford, UK: Oxford University Press.

Miller, M. A. 2011. *Hard Train Slow Train: Passages about Dylan.* Denver, CO: Jupiter Hollow Media.

Mirken, C. 1965. "Newport: The Short Hot Summer." *Broadside,* August 15.

Muir, A. 2001. *Razor's Edge: Bob Dylan and the Never Ending Tour.* London: Helter Skelter.

———. 2003. *Troubadour: Early and Late Songs of Bob Dylan.* Bluntisham, UK: Woodstock Publications.

Negus, K. 2007. "Living, Breathing Songs: Singing along with Bob Dylan." *Oral Tradition* 22(1): 71–83.

———. 2008. *Bob Dylan.* London: Equinox.

Neill, A. 1999. "Inauthenticity, Insincerity, and Poetry." In *Performance and Authenticity in the Arts,* edited by S. Kemal and I. Gaskell, 197–214. Cambridge: Cambridge University Press.

Nielsen, A. L. 2009. "Crow Jane Approximately: Bob Dylan's Black Masque." In *Highway 61 Revisited: Bob Dylan's Road from Minnesota to the World*, edited by C. J. Sheehy and T. Swiss, 186–196. Minneapolis: University of Minnesota Press.

Ochs, P. 1965. "An Open Letter from Phil Ochs." *Broadside* 54, 20 January.

Ottanelli, F. 1991. *The Communist Party of the United States from the Depression to World War Two*. Piscataway, NJ: Rutgers University Press.

Paredez, D. 2009. *Selenidad: Selena, Latinos, and the Performance of Memory*. Durham, NC: Duke University Press.

Pareles, J. 1997. "A Wiser Voice Blowin' in the Autumn Wind." *New York Times*, September 28.

Pattie, D. 2007. *Rock Music in Performance*. Basingstoke, UK: Palgrave-Macmillan.

Paxton, T. 1966. "Folk Rot." *Sing Out!* January.

Peterson, R. 1997. *Creating Country Music: Fabricating Authenticity*. Chicago: University of Chicago Press.

———. 2005. "In Search of Authenticity." *Journal of Management Studies* 42(5): 1083–1098.

Pichaske, D. 2010. *Songs of the North Country: A Midwest Framework to the Songs of Bob Dylan*. New York: Continuum.

Polito, R. 2009. "Bob Dylan's Memory Palace." In *Highway 61 Revisited: Bob Dylan's Road from Minnesota to the World*, edited by C. J. Sheehy and T. Swiss, 140–153. Minneapolis: University of Minnesota Press.

Polizzotti, M. 2006. *Bob Dylan's Highway 61 Revisited*. New York: Continuum.

Randall, A. J. 2008. *Dusty! Queen of the Postmods*. Oxford, UK: Oxford University Press.

Ratcliffe, J. 2011. *Mississippi John Hurt: His Life, His Times, His Blues*. Jackson: University Press of Mississippi.

Redhead, S., and J. Street. 1989. "Have I the Right? Legitimacy, Authenticity and Community in Folk's Politics." *Popular Music* 8(2): 177–184.

Reginio, R. 2009. "Nettie Moore: Minstrelsy and the Cultural Economy of Race in Bob Dylan's Late Albums." In *Highway 61 Revisited: Bob Dylan's Road from Minnesota to the World*, edited by C. J. Sheehy and T. Swiss, 213–224. Minneapolis: University of Minnesota Press.

Richardson, J. T., ed. 1978. *Conversion Careers*. Beverly Hills, CA: Sage.

———. 1985 "The Active vs. Passive Convert." *Journal for the Scientific Study of Religion* 24:163–179.

Ricks, C. 2003. *Dylan's Visions of Sin*. New York: Ecco.

Rodnitzky, J. L. 1976. *Minstrels of the Dawn: The Folk-Protest Singer as a Cultural Hero.* Chicago: Nelson-Hall.

———. 1988. "Also Born in the USA: Bob Dylan's Outlaw Heroes and the Real Bob Dylan." *Popular Music and Society* 12(2): 37–44.

Rogan, J. 1991. *Timeless Flight.* Brentwood, UK: Square One Books.

Roy, W. G. 2010. *Reds, Whites, and Blues: Social Movements, Folk Music, and Race in the United States.* Princeton, NJ: Princeton University Press.

Scaduto, A. 1971. *Bob Dylan: An Intimate Biography.* New York: Grosset and Dunlap.

Schroeder, P. R. 2004. *Robert Johnson, Mythmaking and Contemporary American Culture.* Urbana: University of Illinois Press.

Scobie, S. 2003. *Alias Bob Dylan Revisited.* Calgary, Alberta: Red Deer Press.

Selvin, J. 1979. "Dylan's God-Awful Gospel." *San Francisco Chronicle,* November 3.

Shank, B. 2002. "That Thin Wild Mercury Sound: Bob Dylan and the Illusion of American Culture." *Boundary* 2 29(1): 97–110.

Sheehy, C. J., and T. Swiss, eds. 2009. *Highway 61 Revisited: Bob Dylan's Road from Minnesota to the World.* Minneapolis: University of Minnesota Press.

Shelton, R. 1961. "Bob Dylan: A Distinctive Folk-Song Stylist." *New York Times,* September 29.

———. 1965a. "Beneath the Festival's Razzle-Dazzle." *New York Times,* August 1.

———. 1965b. "The Beatles Will Make the Scene Again, but the Scene Has Changed." *New York Times,* August 11.

———. 1965c. "Dylan Conquers an Unruly Audience." *New York Times,* August 30.

———. 1986. *No Direction Home: The Life and Music of Bob Dylan.* New York: Beech Tree Books.

———. 2004. "Interview with Abe and Beatty Zimmerman (full version)." In *Isis: A Bob Dylan Anthology,* edited by D. Barker, 15–36. London: Helter Skelter.

Shils, E. 1975. *Center and Periphery: Essays in Macro-Sociology.* Chicago: University of Chicago Press.

Silber, I. 1964. "Folk Music and the Success Syndrome." In *The American Folk Scene: Dimensions of the Folksong Revival,* edited by D. De Turk and A. Poulin, 298–302. New York: Dell.

Simmel, G. 1950. "The Stranger." In *The Sociology of Georg Simmel.* 402–408. New York: The Free Press.

Skinner, K. 2006. "Must Be Born Again: Resurrecting the Anthology of American Folk Music." *Popular Music* 25(1): 57–75.

Sloman, L. 2002. *On the Road with Bob Dylan.* New York: Three Rivers Press.

Smart, N. 2009. "Nothing but Affection for All Those Who've Sailed with Me: Bob Dylan from Place to Place." *Popular Music and Society* 32(2): 179–197.

Smith, J. 2010. "A Town Called Riddle: Excavating Todd Haynes' *I'm Not There*." *Screen* 51(1): 71–78.

Smith, L. D. 2002. *Bob Dylan, Bruce Springsteen, and American Song*. Westport, CT: Praeger.

Solis, G. 2010. "I Did It My Way: Rock and the Logic of Covers." *Popular Music and Society* 33(3): 297–318.

Sounes, H. 2001. *Down the Highway: The Life of Bob Dylan*. New York: Grove Press.

Strausbaugh, J. 2007. *Black Like You: Blackface, Whiteface, Insult and Imitation in American Popular Culture*. New York: Tarcher.

Sutton-Smith, B. 1997. *The Ambiguity of Play*. Cambridge, MA: Harvard University Press.

Svedburg, A. 1963. "I Am My Words." *Newsweek*, November 4.

Thompson, T. 2008. *Positively Main Street: Bob Dylan's Minnesota*. Minneapolis: University of Minnesota Press.

Turino, T. 2008. *Music as Social Life: The Politics of Participation*. Chicago: University of Chicago Press.

Turner, V. 1969. *The Ritual Process: Structure and Anti-Structure*. Chicago: Aldine.

———. 1974. *Dramas, Fields, and Metaphors: Symbolic Action in Human Society*. Ithaca, NY: Cornell University Press.

———. 1982. *From Ritual to Theatre: The Human Seriousness of Play*. New York: Performing Arts Journal Publications.

Unterberger, R. 2000. *Turn! Turn! Turn! The '60's Folk-Rock Revolution*. San Francisco, CA: Backbeat Books.

Van Ronk, D. 2005. *The Mayor of McDougal Street*. Cambridge, MA: DaCapo.

Vernezze, P., and C. J. Porter, eds. 2006. *Bob Dylan and Philosophy*. Chicago: Open Court.

Vials, C. 2009. *Realism for the Masses: Aesthetics, Popular Front Pluralism, and U.S. Culture, 1935–1947*. Jackson: University Press of Mississippi.

Webb, S. H. 2006. *Dylan Redeemed: From Highway 61 to Saved*. New York: Continuum.

Wilentz, S. 2003. "American Recordings: On 'Love and Theft' and the Minstrel Boy." In *"Do You, Mr. Jones?" Bob Dylan with the Poets and the Professors*, edited by N. Corcoran, 295–306. London: Pimlico.

———. 2010. *Bob Dylan in America*. New York: Doubleday.

Williams, P. 1980. *Dylan: What Happened?* South Bend, IN: and/ Entwhistle.

———. 1994. *Bob Dylan: Performing Artist 1974–1986: The Middle Years*. London: Omnibus Press.

———. 2004a. *Bob Dylan: Performing Artist 1960–1973: The Early Years.* London: Omnibus Press.

———. 2004b. *Bob Dylan: Performing Artist 1986–1990 and Beyond.* London: Omnibus Press.

Wilson, R. 2009. *Be Always Converting, Be Always Converted: An American Poetics.* Cambridge, MA: Harvard University Press

Witting, R. 2002. *Desire: Songs of Redemption.* Scunthorpe, UK: Exploding Rooster Books.

Wolfe, P. 1964. "The 'New' Dylan." *Broadside* 53, December 20.

Wyman, B. 2005. "Dylan Gives People What He Wants." *New York Times*, June 12.

Yaffe, D. 2011. *Bob Dylan: Like a Complete Unknown.* New Haven, CT: Yale University Press.

◇

Index

◇

About the Author

Andrea Cossu is an independent writer and a sociologist who most recently was a visiting fellow at Yale University. He is the author of several articles on culture and memory, which have appeared in prominent journals and books.